Woman's Day

by Shirley Sarvis

Introduction by Jean Voltz,
Food Editor, Woman's Day

Home Cooking Around the World

SIMON AND SCHUSTER • NEW YORK

DESIGNED BY EVE METZ
MANUFACTURED IN THE UNITED STATES OF AMERICA

1   2   3   4   5   6   7   8   9   10
LIBRARY OF CONGRESS CATALOGING IN PUBLICATION DATA
MAIN ENTRY UNDER TITLE:

WOMAN'S DAY HOME COOKING AROUND THE WORLD.

   INCLUDES INDEX.
   1. COOKERY, INTERNATIONAL.   I. SARVIS, SHIRLEY.
II. WOMAN'S DAY.   III. TITLE HOME COOKING AROUND
THE WORLD.
TX725.A1W62   1977   641.5'9   77-11113
ISBN 0-671-22512-X

Contents

A number of very chic, very expensive restaurants make it a point to serve dishes born in home kitchens. They offer French *poule-au-pot,* Italian vegetable *frittata,* or American corn bread as their specialty. These down-to-earth delights confirm that the best home cooking can rival the best work of a professional chef.

In Argentina you can get fabulous beefsteaks in many of the excellent restaurants. The thick cuts of meat are beautifully broiled and bursting with succulent juices. But such a dinner will not be nearly so tasty or interesting as a sauté of ground beef with onions, garlic, hominy, beans, and herbs as they are cooked in an Argentine home. And the price of the steak, even in Argentina, will far exceed the cost of the ingredients for the home-cooked meal.

Cooking in your own kitchen is not only practical, convenient (since you are there), and good, but it is usually low in cost. It has to be, because there are times when almost every family budget is limited. Budgeting can lead to creativity in the kitchen, and many of the recipes in *Woman's Day Home Cooking Around the World* are included especially for the cook who wants to discover versatility and hearty nutrition at a low cost.

The equation of true home cooking and economy cooking is a happy relationship. Careful preparation and inventive use of a variety of textures, colors, and spices in cooking can actually result in a much better dish. This may be true because the economy-minded cook puts great importance on the selection of the finest ingredients and on the seasoning as well as on the cutting of meats and vegetables for the best results. The extended periods of cooking often required for home dishes may also be partly responsible. Whatever the reason, more of the cook's loving care goes into these home meals, and carefully prepared beef cubes may be better than a whole roast, or a succulent fish soup more satisfying than a whole poached trout.

Budget cooking gives us a good excuse to learn some of the delicious dishes that our counterpart cooks in other countries prepare for their families as staples in their diet. These economical dishes are interesting and intriguing in their variety and invention. While resplendent roasts and elaborate gourmet foods are impressive at first, they pall easily and can become boring. There is certainly more to ponder in an entrée of lean pork sausages and Italian beans with basil and garlic than there is in a crown roast with an elaborate stuffing.

A pleasant aspect of the low-cost home dishes in this collection is that they can inspire a mood. They make for a comfortable ambience. The inviting dishes are not pretentious, and so they seem natural and welcoming. They are like an invitation to immediate delights. They are an open door and a greeting saying, "Come in and enjoy life with us."

About the recipes: Here are some suggestions that might be helpful in understanding how the recipes were prepared and why they were included; also, a few tips about keeping the recipes authentic while at the same time making them your own.

• With most recipes accompaniment suggestions, sometimes an entire menu, are listed. These are ideas only, not requirements for the success of the dish. You might prefer some other wines or side dishes.

• In many cases, these recipes are of international inspiration but adapted for American home kitchens. To do this, many techniques are modified for the American manner of food preparation and cooking and to make them more acceptable to our palates. At the same time, every effort is made to hold to the intention of each recipe. For example, we do not suggest that you boil a chicken for two hours, as in the traditional Tunisian recipe, since our tender birds do not require a long cooking time. But we have kept all the other ingredients and the use of traditional Tunisian spices. Our American tastes in fish tend toward a more delicate result than is popular in France; we have honored our tastes. The fact that an authentic Swiss mountain-village recipe uses rather thick pancakes and chunks of onions in sauce does not mean that Americans want the same heartiness. So we use thinner crêpes and substitute minced green onions in the sauce, which seems more compatible with our preferences.

Introduction

Selecting from many sources and adapting dishes to our own style of cooking is characteristic of American cuisine. That happens in this book.

Today, in this country, we are probably able to make a wider variety of dishes than can be created anywhere else in the world. This is because of our diverse and excellent ingredients and our streamlined techniques for every kind of cooking process. Our methods do not require the original cooking techniques, which are often slow and complicated, to produce the same dishes. Another advantage is that we can still get the best food values for our dollar: in quality and consistency the produce is extraordinary.

How fortunate we are to be able to draw from delicious home dishes from countries and cultures all over the world and to make them and enjoy them here. So have an international trip tonight—without leaving your own home or your own kitchen.

JEANNE VOLTZ

Sufficient Soups

If you think of soup suppers as not substantial, banish the thought. These soups are sufficient enough in themselves to be the main part of a meal. Many of them are almost stews.

Almost anywhere, I find that if soup is to be supper, the meal is usually a rather hearty affair. The cooks tend to try to make up for the unmighty concept of soup with big bounties of accompaniments—good breads, hearty cheeses, plump desserts, or significant salads.

I find that a good soup has a looseness about it that seems to open up and air flavors. Perhaps this is another reason I find such satisfaction in a soup supper.

My main soup advisories:

A soup can soar no higher than its stock.

A freshly made soup always tastes best. A too-often-reheated soup tastes too-often-reheated.

MR. AARON'S FRESH MUSHROOM SOUP

USA

*Nat Aaron is a retired lawyer and a dedicated and knowl-
edgeable food shopper and cook. I tremendously admire his
style of cooking, which comes not from books but from ex-
perience. He suggests, "Get the best food you can and treat
it simply and kindly; then accompany it so that there is
pleasure in eating and a good feeling afterward." His is a
dashing mushroom soup. Or you might say it is a leek-and-
potato soup far out of its own class. It is nearly burdened
with chewy and crisp fresh mushrooms. The curry should
not be a definable taste; it should only point up the other
flavors.*

*Mr. and Mrs. Aaron sprinkle their soup with a little
freshly grated Parmesan cheese. I do not; I prefer, instead,
to float a sprig of parsley on top of each serving for color.*

> 2 *quarts homemade chicken broth (made with a generous
> amount of onion and celery in the seasoning), strained,
> and all fat removed*
> 1-*pound mature (baking) potato, peeled and finely diced*
> 1 *cup sliced leeks (white part only)*
> *Curry powder*
> 1½ *pounds fresh mushrooms, thickly sliced*
> *Salt and freshly ground black pepper*

Combine broth, potato, leeks, and ¼ teaspoon curry powder in a
kettle. Cover and gently boil until vegetables are tender, about
10 minutes. Add mushrooms, cover, and gently boil until mushrooms are just tender, about 10 minutes. Put mixture into blender
container (in two or three portions if necessary) and whirl *just* for
a moment, until mushrooms are cut to about ¼-inch dice. Correct seasoning with salt, pepper, and additional curry. Reheat
if necessary. Makes about 2 quarts or 4 luncheon servings.

SUGGESTED ACCOMPANIMENTS:
Buttered broil-toasted crisp English muffins
White table wine

POTATO, GREENS, AND SAUSAGE SOUP
(Caldo Verde)   PORTUGAL

The skill of a Portuguese cook is sometimes judged by the fineness with which kale is stripped for caldo verde. *Our kale is not identical to Portuguese kale, but you can use fresh spinach or very green outer lettuce leaves or even cabbage.*

A country corn bread is the essential accompaniment in Portugal, and it should be served here also. So should a lively dry red table wine.

> 4 *to* 6 *ounces* linguiça *or Polish sausages or other smoked pork garlic sausages, casings removed if necessary*
> 1½ *pounds potatoes, peeled and sliced*
> 1½ *teaspoons salt*
> ½ *cup olive oil*
>   *About* ¼ *teaspoon freshly ground black pepper*
> 6 *ounces fresh spinach or green lettuce or cabbage (heavy stems removed before weighing), washed, gathered together, and cut into strips as fine as possible*

Pierce sausages in three places with a fork, cover with cold water, heat to boiling, simmer for 15 minutes, drain, and cut into ¼-inch slices. Put potatoes, 5 cups water, and salt into a heavy kettle, cover, and gently boil until potatoes are tender. Remove potatoes, mash until smooth, and return to kettle. Add oil, pepper, and sausages and heat to boiling. Add greens and boil, uncovered, just until tender, about 3 minutes. Add additional salt if necessary. Makes 4 main-course servings.

MULLIGATAWNY SOUP

INDIA

When you correct the seasoning at the end, take into account that mulligatawny means "pepper water." The soup ought to carry out this meaning with some heat in the taste.

3-pound frying chicken, cut into serving pieces
4 cups water
Salt
¾ cup finely chopped onions
2½ teaspoons powdered turmeric
2 teaspoons ground coriander
1½ teaspoons poppy seeds
Cayenne
5 tablespoons butter
2 large pressed cloves garlic
½ cup sifted all-purpose flour
1 small can (about 8 ounces) garbanzos
Ground cloves
Freshly ground black pepper
Minced fresh parsley
Hot cooked rice
Moist flaked or grated fresh coconut

In a kettle, simmer chicken with water and 1½ teaspoons salt until tender, about 45 minutes to 1 hour. Remove chicken and save broth. In a large kettle over medium heat, sauté onions, turmeric, coriander, poppy seeds, and a pinch of cayenne in butter until onions are tender. Remove from heat and stir in garlic and flour. Whirl garbanzos with their liquid in a blender until smooth; add to onions. Return kettle to heat and gradually whisk in reserved chicken stock. Simmer, whisking frequently, for 15 minutes. Whisk in ⅛ teaspoon ground cloves. Return chicken to kettle and heat through. Taste and correct seasoning with salt, cayenne, cloves, and pepper. Ladle into bowls. Sprinkle very lightly with parsley. Pass rice and coconut to be added to taste. Makes 4 servings.

SUGGESTED ACCOMPANIMENTS:
Fresh cucumber spears
Lightly cooked spinach salad or tender leaf spinach-and-lettuce salad
Crisp cracker bread or Indian wafers
Light beer or a dry California Sauvignon Blanc

SWEDISH SPLIT-PEA SOUP

SWEDEN

Serve this soup with rye bread and beer and a big green salad, finishing off with crisp red apples.

1½ *pounds meaty ham hocks, sawed into 1-inch-thick pieces*
2 *quarts cold water*
1½ *cups dried yellow split peas, rinsed*
1 *cup finely chopped onions*
2 *carrots, peeled and thinly sliced*
1 *stalk celery, thinly sliced*
⅛ *teaspoon crumbled dried thyme*
Salt and freshly ground black pepper
Finely chopped fresh parsley

Put ham and water into a large kettle. Cover and simmer for 1 hour. Add peas, onions, carrots, celery, and thyme. Cover and simmer until peas are very tender, about 1½ hours; stir occasionally. Remove ham, discard bones, and break up large pieces of ham. Whirl vegetable liquid in a blender until smooth; return to kettle. Return ham to kettle and heat through. Add salt and pepper to taste. Sprinkle lightly with parsley. Makes 4 generous servings.

SOUP OF THE MORNING

ECUADOR

In Ecuador, I was told, "After a big night, at three or four in the morning, people eat this to feel strong." That does not preclude its being served at a more seemly hour, say between six and eight in the evening.

If you serve boiled potatoes with the soup, each person can cut bites of potato into his soup if he wishes.

The cook who gave me this recipe cautioned, "Your onions must not show in your soup."

3 meaty center-cut beef shanks, each at least ½ pound and
 1 inch thick
 Olive oil
 Salt and freshly ground black pepper
1 cup grated or finely minced onions (1 large onion)
3 pressed cloves garlic
5 cups water
1 green bell pepper, chopped
1 cup salted roasted peanuts, ground
 About ¾ teaspoon ground cumin
 About ⅛ teaspoon crushed dried hot red peppers
1 can (14½ ounces) golden hominy, drained
1 small jar (2 ounces) sliced pimientos
 Parsley Sauce (recipe below)

In a heavy, large kettle, brown shanks well in a small amount of oil; remove and season very generously with salt and pepper. Add more oil if necessary to make 2 tablespoons of drippings in kettle.

Add onions and sauté until tender. Return meat to kettle and add garlic and water. Heat to boiling, simmer for 5 minutes, and skim off film that may form on top. Add green pepper, peanuts, cumin, and red peppers. Cover and simmer until meat is very tender, about 2 hours. Remove shanks, discard bones and connective tissue, break meat into 1- by ½-inch pieces, and return to kettle along with hominy and pimientos. Heat through. Correct seasoning with salt and pepper. Ladle into shallow soup plates. Pass parsley sauce to be spooned into soup. Makes 6 servings.

Parsley Sauce. Stir together ⅔ cup olive oil, ⅔ cup finely chopped fresh parsley, 3 tablespoons minced green onions (white part only), 1 teaspoon salt, and 2 tablespoons fresh lemon juice.

SUGGESTED ACCOMPANIMENTS:
Avocado, orange, lettuce salad
Boiled potatoes or crusty bread
Light beer

CHICKEN-AND-MINT SOUP
(Canja à Brasileira)   BRAZIL

3½-*pound chicken, cut into serving pieces*
  2 *quarts water*
    Salt and freshly ground black pepper
  1 *large onion, peeled and quartered*
  1 *large parsley sprig*
  1 *large clove garlic, peeled and split*
  2 *large carrots, peeled and thinly sliced*
  ¼ *pound well-smoked ham, torn or cut into fine slivers*
  ½ *cup long-grain white rice*
    1 *cup dices of peeled and seeded ripe tomatoes (optional)*
    About ¼ cup finely chopped fresh parsley
    About ¼ cup minced fresh mint leaves

Put into a large kettle the chicken, water, 1½ teaspoons salt, ¼ teaspoon pepper, onion, parsley sprig, and garlic. Heat to boiling, then simmer, covered, until chicken is tender, about 1 hour. Remove chicken and remove skin (if you wish) and bones. Break meat into large pieces. Strain broth and return to kettle. Return chicken to broth. (Chill if you wish and remove excess fat on top.) Add carrots, ham, and rice. Cover and simmer until rice and carrots are tender, about 30 minutes. Add tomatoes and heat through. Season generously with salt and pepper. Sprinkle with chopped parsley and mint. Makes 6 servings.

SUGGESTED ACCOMPANIMENTS:

Corn bread
Avocado and tender leaf lettuce salad (optional)
Fresh pineapple
Dry white wine

DUST-BOWL SOUP

USA

In the days when San Francisco firemen worked twenty-four-hour shifts, Larry Crabtree could put this soup on to simmer at eight in the morning and have it ready for his company at six o'clock suppertime. The name that Larry bestowed on this soup hints at his Oklahoma origin. The soup's spiciness makes it right for cold-weather nights.

You may be able to get by with less simmering, but Larry said to do it this way, so I always do. I depart from Larry's instructions in one way: I base the soup on browned beef bones rather than uncooked ones. When possible, I use prime-rib bones left from a roast. Or I get beef bones and brown them in a 450° oven, turning once, for 30 minutes. (I can still get beef bones free from my meatman. I hope that you can too. It makes for such a low-cost start.)

    2 *to* 3 *pounds browned beef bones (directions above; or*
    use well-washed uncooked bones)
    9 *cups cold water*
    ½ *cup dry black-eyed peas*
    ½ *cup dry pinto beans*
    ⅛ *teaspoon crushed dried red peppers*
    1½ *cups chopped onions*
    ¾ *cup chopped celery*
    1 *large celery top sprig*
    1 *medium-sized potato, peeled and finely diced*
    1 *large pressed clove garlic*
    1 *tablespoon salt*
    1 *bay leaf*
    2 *teaspoons chili powder*
    ⅛ *teaspoon freshly ground black pepper*
    Chopped parsley or a few green peas (optional)

Put bones and water into a large kettle. Bring to a boil, then cover and simmer very slowly for 2 hours. Add black-eyed peas, beans, and red peppers. Cover and simmer for 6 hours or more. Cool until fat rises to top. Skim off fat. Add remaining ingredients, except parsley or peas, cover, and simmer until vegetables are tender, about 1 hour. Remove bones and bay leaf. Correct seasoning with salt and pepper. To add color, sprinkle with a touch of chopped parsley or add a few green peas near the end of cooking time. Makes 4 generous main-course servings.

SUGGESTED ACCOMPANIMENTS:
Crusty corn bread or French-style bread
Aged Monterey Jack or Cheddar cheese
Red wine

PORK-AND-HOMINY SOUP
(Pozole) MEXICO

I especially like this soup because it is so wholesome, yet refreshing and intriguing because of all the possible flavors with which you can experiment. As a mainstay soup in Mexico, pozole gets many different interpretations. You may make your own interpretation as you choose condiments to add—some, or maybe all, of these: fresh lime juice, onions, hot red peppers, avocados, shredded lettuce, oregano, radishes.

2½-*pound fresh boneless pork-shoulder-blade Boston roast*
(boneless pork butt)
3 *quarts cold water*
1½ *cups finely chopped onions*
Salt
1 *pound chicken legs and thighs*
1 *large can (1 pound, 13 ounces) white hominy, drained*
Liberal amounts of condiments:
Small limes, cut in half top to bottom, or large limes, cut into wedges
Thinly sliced green onions with part of green tops
Crushed dried hot red peppers
Peeled ripe avocados, cut into slender arcs or dices
Iceberg lettuce, sliced into shred-strips
Snipped fresh or crumbled dried leaf oregano
Finely diced red radishes

Put pork, water, onions, and 1½ tablespoons salt into a large kettle. Cover and simmer for 2 hours. Add chicken and hominy, and simmer until meats are very tender, about 1 hour. Remove meats. Chill soup, then skim off fat. Meantime, remove any fat, bones, and skin from meats, tear meats into fine strips, and return to soup. Near serving time, reheat soup and add salt to taste.

Ladle into large shallow soup plates. Pass condiments. Makes 8 servings.

SUGGESTED ACCOMPANIMENTS:
Tostaditas
Beer

CARROT GOLDEN BISQUE

USA

The basic soup idea comes from a famous restaurant. The pork and pepper additions are mine.

6 *cups chicken broth*
6 *carrots, peeled and very thinly sliced*
¼ *cup chopped onions*
1 *peeled clove garlic*
   Ground nutmeg
¼ *cup heavy (whipping) cream*
1½ *tablespoons creamy peanut butter*
2 *teaspoons Worcestershire sauce*
   Generous dash of hot-pepper sauce
¾ *pound leftover roast or boiled pork, finely diced*
   Salt and freshly ground black pepper
¼ *cup very fine dices of green bell peppers*
   About 1 cup commercial sour cream at room temperature

In a kettle combine the broth, carrots, onions, garlic, and ¼ teaspoon nutmeg. Cover and gently boil until carrots are very tender. Turn into blender container and whirl until smooth. Add cream, peanut butter, Worcestershire, and hot-pepper sauce; whirl again. Return to kettle, add pork, and heat through. Season generously with salt and pepper. Ladle into warm bowls. Sprinkle each serving with green peppers, top with a spoonful of sour cream, and sprinkle with nutmeg. Makes 3 supper servings.

SUGGESTED ACCOMPANIMENTS:
Large crisp sesame wafers
Red apples
Dry white table wine or light beer

AVOCADO SOUP, OAXACA

MEXICO

To make this soup sing out its freshness, use only ripe, sweet tomatoes, and chop the coriander just before serving. Offer coarse salt and additional coriander to add to taste.

> 1 *whole chicken breast (about 1 pound), split*
> *Cold water*
> 2 *teaspoons salt*
> 1/8 *teaspoon crushed dried red peppers*
> 2 *ripe avocados, peeled and cut into 2- by 1/4-inch strips*
> 1 1/4 *cups coarse dices of peeled and seeded ripe tomatoes*
> 1 1/2 *cups coarsely chopped fresh coriander* (cilantro)

Cover chicken with water, gently boil for 5 minutes, drain, and rinse. In a covered kettle, simmer together chicken, 6 cups water, salt, and red pepper until chicken is very tender, about 30 minutes. Bone and skin chicken. Tear flesh into strips about 2 by 1/4 inch. For each serving: Arrange one-fourth of the chicken, avocados, and tomatoes in separate mounds in bottom of a large shallow soup plate; sprinkle with coriander. Heat broth to boiling and pour over mounds in soup plates. Serve immediately. Makes 4 servings.

Sufficient Soups

SUGGESTED ACCOMPANIMENTS:
Warm corn tortillas
Fresh radishes
Cold beer

The Salads of Plenty

For years, ladies have been making club luncheons of a salad and a hot bread. And they have done it extremely well. That combination almost always entails mutual flattery.

But that joining does not have to be the exclusive property of the ladies. Neither do we have to keep thinking of salads as only prettied-up and inconsequential things for leisure ladies' noontimes. Salads can be big and bold and central to a supper.

The best way that I can applaud the ladies' good notion is to continue it and expand on it in heartier ways, sometimes with huskier salads and breads.

I do not know that the ladies have ever eschewed wine with their salads. Salad and bread and wine make an excellent combination. Sometimes try beer instead of wine.

ISAR SUMMER SALAD

GERMANY

½ *pound fine-quality sliced bologna, cut into strips 2 inches
   long and ⅛ inch wide*
2 *medium-sized cucumbers (one peeled and one unpeeled),
   halved, lengthwise and thinly sliced crosswise*
1 *cup thinly sliced red radishes*
1 *green bell pepper, quartered lengthwise and very thinly
   sliced crosswise*
⅓ *cup minced green onions with part of green tops*
   About ¼ cup olive oil
   About ¼ cup red wine vinegar
   About 1½ teaspoons salt
   About ¾ teaspoon freshly ground black pepper

Combine bologna, cucumbers, radishes, green pepper, and onions
in a salad bowl. Toss with enough oil to coat all ingredients.
Sprinkle with vinegar and salt and pepper to taste, and toss again.
Makes 4 main-course servings.

SUGGESTED ACCOMPANIMENTS:
Fresh crusty French-style rolls
Cold beer

HOT PINE-NUT CRISP CABBAGE

FRANCE

*A good friend, Dottie Adamson, gave me this recipe idea,
and her note of warning compels attention: This dish is a
disaster if you cook the cabbage any longer than the recipe
says!*

This also works well as a salad course for a dinner, espe-

cially when you want to keep drinking red wine after a meat course and through the salad course.

> 2 *pounds green cabbage (small head)*
> 6 *tablespoons butter*
> ½ *cup toasted pine nuts*
>> *About ¾ teaspoon salt*
>> *About ½ teaspoon freshly ground black pepper*
>> *About ½ teaspoon sugar*

Break cabbage leaves into pieces about 2 inches square. Drop all at once into a large kettle of boiling salted water. Stir and cook for 30 to 60 seconds only (cabbage should just turn bright green and heat through and keep its crisp sweetness). Immediately drain very well. Meantime, heat butter until it foams and richly browns. Toss cabbage with butter, nuts, and salt, pepper, and sugar to taste. Serve immediately. Makes 3 main-course or 6 salad servings.

SUGGESTED ACCOMPANIMENTS:
Cheeses (fairly mild)
French bread
Red apples
Light dry red wine or beer

WHITE BEANS WITH TUNA
(Fagioli al Tonno)   ITALY

Serve two salads, this and a green one, both dressed with oil and vinegar.

> 2 *cans (7 ounces each) solid white tuna with oil, broken into large chunks*
> 2 *cups cooked dry small white beans (Great Northerns)*
> 4 *large ripe tomatoes, peeled, seeded, and coarsely chopped*
>> *About ¼ cup olive oil*

   2 *large pressed cloves garlic*
     Salt and freshly ground black pepper
     Red wine vinegar
   1 *cup finely chopped fresh basil leaves (chop and add*
     the basil just before serving)

Put tuna with oil, beans, and tomatoes into a salad bowl. Sprinkle with olive oil, garlic, 2 teaspoons salt, ½ teaspoon pepper, and 3 tablespoons vinegar. Gently toss to mix well. Correct seasoning with salt, pepper, and vinegar. Sprinkle with basil. Pass additional vinegar. Makes 4 servings.

   NOTE: To cook beans with a quick-soak method, rinse beans, generously cover with cold water, boil for 2 minutes, remove from heat, cover, and let stand for 1 hour. Lightly salt, loosely cover, and simmer until tender, adding more water if necessary to keep beans covered.

   SUGGESTED ACCOMPANIMENTS:
Green salad
Warm bread sticks
Bright dry red wine such as a California Grignolino or a young
   Italian Chianti
Lemon sherbet or ice with Italian biscotti or fresh pears

CHICKEN SALAD MONTEIL

TRINIDAD

The cooks of Port-of-Spain know how to boost a hometown product. They use bitters by the teaspoon instead of the drop. This bitters seasoning is subtle and unusual.

   2 *cups diced cooked chicken*
   1 *cup diced celery*

2½ tablespoons minced green onions with part of green tops
½ cup coarsely chopped walnuts
1½ tablespoons finely chopped fresh parsley
    Rum Dressing (recipe below)
    Salt and freshly ground black pepper
    Broken soft-leaf lettuce

In bowl combine chicken, celery, onions, nuts, and parsley. Gently toss with dressing. Correct seasoning using a generous amount of salt and pepper. Serve on plates lined with lettuce. Makes 4 servings.

Rum Dressing. Beat together with a fork until smooth ⅓ cup mayonnaise, 2 teaspoons medium (golden) rum, 2 teaspoons fresh lime juice, ¾ teaspoon bitters, ½ teaspoon Dijon-style mustard, ⅛ teaspoon salt, and ⅛ teaspoon freshly ground black pepper.

SUGGESTED ACCOMPANIMENTS:
Toasted corn bread
Fruity white wine

RAHELA'S ROASTED RED PEPPERS
YUGOSLAVIA

Rahela is a wondrous woman and cook in Dubrovnik. I got a chance to watch her cook and to eat at her splendid table for a week one summer. Those were days of the most luxurious eating that I ever expect to have. The luxury came not from excess fanciness but from the rich satisfaction of natural flavors and the care and artistry that went into that food. The overpowering qualities of Rahela's food were freshness and naturalness—but with utter tastiness.

The fall red peppers in this dish are sweet and full of rich flavor. After roasting and peeling, some charred bits of

skin cling to the outside and add a special spiciness. When
the peppers are dressed and finished, you get the full effect
of juicy fleshiness along with an inviting bitterness, a ripe
sweetness, and a scintillating hotness. Side with small grilled
fish—whatever is abundant and inexpensive.

4 *large red bell peppers*
 About ½ teaspoon salt (preferably coarse)
1 *very large pressed clove garlic*
2 *tablespoons olive oil*
1 *tablespoon mild white wine vinegar*
 Butter-lettuce leaves

Wash and dry peppers. Place on a tray about 2 inches below pre-
heated broiler. Broil, turning, until well blistered and charred on
all sides. As each pepper is finished, place in a kettle and cover
tightly. Let peppers rest until cool enough to handle. The peppers seem easier to peel if you let them cool and steam for an
hour or more—until nearly room temperature. Gently peel with
fingertips; try not to tear flesh. Place whole peppers in a bowl.
Sprinkle with salt, garlic, oil, and vinegar; turn peppers to season
and coat on all sides. Let stand for at least 30 minutes; or cover
and chill for a day or more. Serve the peppers with all juices on
a few leaves of soft butter lettuce. Makes 2 servings.

SUGGESTED ACCOMPANIMENTS:
French-style bread
Fresh dry white wine

DALMATIAN TUNA SALAD

YUGOSLAVIA

*When I first had this in Dubrovnik, served as a first-course
pâté, I felt that dry sherry was right with it. Now that I*

serve the salad as a main course, I still want sherry with it. If that seems too strange, have white wine or beer. Eat this salad with a fork or pile it lavishly onto sesame wafers or toast.

1 *large can (9½ ounces) white tuna*
6 *tablespoons soft butter*
3 *pressed cloves garlic*
1½ *carrots, peeled and grated as finely as possible*
6 *tablespoons coarsely grated dill pickle*
4 *tablespoons coarsely grated sweet onion*
2 *tablespoons coarsely grated red bell pepper, removing skin as you grate (optional)*
6 *tablespoons finely chopped fresh parsley*
About 1½ teaspoons sugar
About ¾ teaspoon freshly ground black pepper
Salt
Lettuce leaves
Ripe olives
Parsley sprigs

Turn tuna with oil into a salad bowl and flake finely with a fork. Mix butter in thoroughly. Add next 9 ingredients. Toss with a fork to mix well. Correct seasoning with salt, sugar, and pepper. Cover and chill thoroughly. Arrange each salad with a border of lettuce leaves and a garnish of ripe olives and parsley sprigs. Makes 4 servings.

SUGGESTED ACCOMPANIMENTS:
Large sesame wafers or thin toast slices
Fresh tomatoes or fresh tomato soup
Dry sherry, or a full and dry white table wine, or beer

WALNUT SALAD MIMOSA

FRANCE

This is a very mellow salad. The spice is in the walnuts. It goes well with wine.

2 quarts broken very tender butter-lettuce leaves
(loosely pack to measure)
¾ cup very finely sliced walnuts, lightly toasted
6 tablespoons minced fresh parsley
Mustard Dressing (recipe below)
8 hard-cooked eggs
Mayonnaise (recipe below, or your own homemade or
quality commercial)
Very thinly sliced smoked ham (optional)

Toss lettuce, ½ cup of the nuts, and half of the parsley with enough mustard dressing to moisten well. Arrange on 4 chilled plates. Halve 6 of the eggs, lengthwise, and embed 3 halves, curved side down, in each salad. Sprinkle eggs lightly with salt and spread generously with mayonnaise. Finely chop remaining eggs and sprinkle over mayonnaise. Sprinkle with remaining nuts and parsley. Garnish with ham, if desired. Makes 4 servings.

Mustard Dressing. Beat together 2 teaspoons mild red wine vinegar, 1 teaspoon Dijon-style mustard, ⅜ teaspoon salt, ¼ teaspoon sugar, ¼ teaspoon freshly ground black pepper, and a dash of Tabasco. Gradually beat in ½ cup olive oil.

Mayonnaise. Place in blender container 1 egg, ¼ cup olive oil, 2 tablespoons fresh lemon juice, 1 teaspoon Dijon-style mustard, a dash of hot-pepper sauce, and ⅜ teaspoon salt. Whirl at high speed until smooth. Remove small part of blender top and slowly pour in ¾ cup more olive oil, continuing to whirl the mixture until smooth and thick.

SUGGESTED ACCOMPANIMENTS:
Whole wheat toast strips
Fruity Gewürztraminer or Riesling

FRANZ'S SWISS CHEESE SALAD

SWITZERLAND

The sharp cheese is the main flavor here, not the dressing. If you want to fatten up this meal, grill some garlic sausages (knackwurst) or frankfurters to serve alongside. Offer mustard.

⅔ *cup mayonnaise*
   About 1 teaspoon white wine vinegar
   About ½ teaspoon freshly ground black pepper
   Freshly grated or ground nutmeg
1 *pound well-aged sharp natural Emmenthal Swiss cheese, cut into ⅛- to ¼-inch dice*
2 *to 3 tablespoons snipped fresh chives*
   Butter-lettuce leaves

Stir together mayonnaise, vinegar, pepper, and ¼ teaspoon nutmeg to make a dressing. Toss cheese and chives with *just* enough dressing to moisten (cheese should be quite dry). Mound each serving on lettuce leaves, sprinkle with more nutmeg, and with more black pepper if you wish. Makes 6 servings.

SUGGESTED ACCOMPANIMENTS:
Caraway seeded rye buns or bread
Cucumber pickles
Tomatoes
Beer

ALBUFEIRA SQUID SALAD

PORTUGAL

The Portuguese put olive oil, vinegar, salt, and pepper on the table to allow for seasoning adjustment. You might

The Salads of Plenty

want to follow the custom. Serve the salad in shallow bowls or scooped plates.

Good cook Belle Rhodes taught me this innovative way to prepare squid, mentioned below. To my mind, it is much more satisfactory than the usual crosswise slicing into rings. The julienne strips curl as they cook. The only way I know to tell when the squid is al dente *is to taste. Begin testing just as soon as the water returns to a boil after adding squid.*

1 *pound fresh squid, prepared as directed below*
4 *medium-sized ripe tomatoes, peeled, seeded, and cut into*
   ½-*inch dices*
6 *tablespoons finely chopped sweet red onions*
6 *tablespoons finely chopped green bell peppers*
4 *tablespoons finely chopped fresh parsley*
2 *tablespoons chopped fresh coriander* (cilantro) *leaves*
   (optional)
4 *tablespoons olive oil*
4 *teaspoons mild red wine vinegar*
   About ¾ *teaspoon salt*
   About ¼ *teaspoon freshly ground black pepper*

Combine all ingredients and gently turn to mix. Cover and chill if you wish. Makes 2 or 3 main-course servings.

Prepared Squid. Wash each squid under running water; remove the speckled membrane that encases the hood and pull off the fins. Pull the head and tentacles from the hood, and cut off and save the tentacles. Slit hood lengthwise and discard contents, including the transparent shell, or sword. Wash hood and tentacles well and rinse in water acidulated with a little lemon juice. Cut hood into ⅛-inch lengthwise julienne strips. Drop strips and tentacles into a large kettle of briskly boiling water, and boil just until tender and *al dente,* about 30 seconds after water returns to boiling. Immediately drain and rinse under cold running water to stop cooking, and drain well again.

SUGGESTED ACCOMPANIMENTS:
French-style bread
Light beer

COOL CUCUMBER-RADISH BOWL

DENMARK

This will not quite make it in heft for a supper main dish, but it makes a great lunch with cold beer and buttered brown or caraway rye bread. Add hard-cooked eggs if you wish and maybe mildly flavored cold cuts.

4 *large regular cucumbers* or 2 *large English cucumbers, peeled and very thinly sliced*
  Salt
2 *cups very thinly sliced washed red radishes*
⅔ *cup heavy (whipping) cream*
3 *tablespoons distilled white vinegar*
2 *teaspoons sugar*
  Freshly ground white pepper

Toss cucumbers with 2 teaspoons salt. Let stand at room temperature for 30 minutes. Rinse well in cold running water, drain, and gently press or squeeze out excess liquid. Cover and chill for 2 hours. Drain off any accumulated moisture. Add radishes. Pour on cream and vinegar, and sprinkle with sugar and a grinding of pepper. Gently toss thoroughly. Add salt if necessary. Serve immediately or cover and chill for 30 minutes. Makes 4 luncheon salad servings.

AUNT MAUD'S WILTED LETTUCE

USA

This is the classic wilted lettuce for me because it is the first I knew and the one I adored all through those young years of hot-evening, summertime suppers in Kansas. In those days, our lettuce was freshly plucked from either our garden or Aunt Maud's.

I still think that a big bowl of this lettuce makes a gorgeous main dish for a summer supper, along with hot corn bread and butter and sliced ripe garden tomatoes.

10 *cups coarsely broken leaf lettuce (loosely pack to measure)*
 4 *ounces bacon, cut into small pieces*
¼ *cup distilled white vinegar*
 2 *tablespoons water*
¼ *teaspoon salt*
⅛ *teaspoon freshly ground black pepper*
⅛ *teaspoon sugar*

Put lettuce into a salad bowl. In a frying pan, slowly cook bacon until crisp. Remove with slotted spoon, drain on paper towels, and add to lettuce. Remove from pan any drippings in excess of ¼ cup. Add vinegar, water, salt, pepper, and sugar to frying pan. Bring to a boil, stirring, and boil until mixture is slightly reduced, about 2 minutes. Pour hot dressing over lettuce. Cover bowl for 30 seconds. Toss lettuce lightly and thoroughly. Serve immediately. Makes 2 main-course or 4 salad servings.

POPPY-SEED ROLLS FOR CHEESE
(Birkes) DENMARK

Not the salad, but the bread to go with the salad.
No wonder the Danes like their cheese—when they tuck

it into poppy-seed rolls designed just for it. These rolls are popular all over Denmark, usually served as a midmorning snack with coffee. I suggest offering them for lunch or supper with a choice of Danish cheeses, beer, and a big lettuce salad. If you want to increase the meal, toss some tiny shrimp with the salad.

I am partial to Danish Tybo as my cheese choice, but Danbo, Havarti, Esrom, and others are excellent too. So is a double layering of a Danish Swiss (Svenbo) and cream cheese. Whatever the cheeses, arrange as thin slices overlapping on a roll: the more surface, the more flavor.

For yeast rolls, these are remarkably fast to make. They bake with a layer of butter in the middle to make top and bottom layers easy to separate to add the cheeses of your choice. Serve these rolls freshly baked and while still a little warm or just cooled.

1 *cup milk*
3 *packages active dry yeast*
3 *cups sifted all-purpose flour*
1 *tablespoon sugar*
1 *teaspoon salt*
10 *tablespoons soft butter*
6 *tablespoons cold butter*
1 *egg white, lightly beaten*
2 *tablespoons poppy seeds*

Scald milk; cool to lukewarm. Sprinkle in yeast, let soften, then stir to dissolve. Sift flour, sugar, and salt together into a large mixing bowl. Cut in soft butter until particles are fine. Stir in yeast mixture. Turn out onto a lightly floured board and knead until dough is smooth and elastic, about 5 minutes. Turn dough to coat with butter in a large buttered bowl, cover with a damp cloth, and let rise in a warm place for 20 to 30 minutes. Punch dough down. Roll out on a lightly floured board to a 20- by 8-inch rectangle. Thinly slice cold butter and place on a lengthwise half of the dough. Fold unbuttered dough over buttered dough, lapping edge under to seal. Brush top with egg white, and sprinkle with poppy seeds. Cut crosswise into 12 slices. Place on an ungreased baking sheet. Bake in a 400° oven until golden brown, about 15 minutes. Cool partially or completely on a rack. Makes 12 rolls, enough for sandwiches for 4 to 6 lunch or supper servings.

Mostly Eggs

My first trip to Europe was a rather long one, taken shortly after I finished school. It was marked by keen budget cautiousness. The trip included driving a chartreuse Volkswagen in and out of cities and countrysides from as far north as Trondheim and Leningrad to as far south as Naples and Barcelona.

Early along the way, I learned how to order safely in any restaurant at any meal in any language, and without doing irreparable damage to my pocketbook. Order an omelet.

In any language, no matter how badly mispronounced, the concept of a delicious treatment for eggs seemed to come across, whether in a desolate mountainside inn in the eerie high Spanish Pyrenees or in a plush Copenhagen restaurant. The "omelet" renditions were always agreeable, remarkably diverse, and often exquisite.

I shall never forget a before-bed supper in remotest German-speaking Switzerland. I had put myself into a dark and decaying little house offering a zimmer for rent. The room itself was made up with clean linens, but it seemed questionable whether this house would make it through the night—with floorboards that creaked as they bent under every step, ancient pieces of country furniture easing themselves apart, and a grotesque stuffed hawk with horrid, dust-

coated black feathers looking down at me from its hideous perch atop the armoire.

Downstairs for supper, I found a cold and damp room with a single round wood table, a worn rag rug on the stone floor, a huge police-type dog pounding its massive billylike tail on the floor, and a weary housewife wondering what I wished to eat. How could I possibly communicate without knowing any German? I retreated to my magic word and brightly flashed "Omelet." My hostess gave a wan smile that possibly meant understanding, then she disappeared, leaving me to wonder what weird thing I might soon be required to eat. More than a few minutes passed. Then came my lady bearing a big platter filled to the edge and over with the most splendid sweet-butter, rippled, eggy crêpe, with sugared fresh strawberries plumping it fat and full. Despite my earlier misgivings, it was delicious because it had been elegantly prepared. So you see, you never know what wonders eggs (and good cooks) can do for you.

Those invariable successes during that trip taught me an unwavering devotion to eggs, especially when the budget needs an assist.

FARMER'S OMELET

Do not rush the crisp-frying of bacon and potato in this recipe.

> 6 *ounces thick-sliced bacon, cut into 2-inch lengths*
> 1 *medium-large potato (about ½ pound), peeled,*
>   *quartered lengthwise, and very thinly sliced*
> 1¼ *cups thinly sliced green onions with part of green tops*
>   8 *eggs*
>   3 *tablespoons cream or milk*
>   *About ½ teaspoon each salt and freshly ground*
>   *black pepper*
> ¼ *teaspoon ground allspice (optional)*

In a large, heavy frying pan over medium heat, cook bacon and potato until both are very crisp, turning as necessary. Discard any drippings in excess of ¼ cup. Add onions and sauté to coat with drippings. Lightly beat eggs with cream, salt, pepper, and, if desired, ground allspice; pour into pan. As eggs begin to set, push and turn in large pieces to softly scramble, keeping them moist. Makes 4 servings.

Another version of this omelet is to fold the crisp bacon, potato, and onions into four individual two-egg French omelets. Then you get the ultimate crispness of potato and bacon. (For French omelet recipe, see Crouton Omelet, page 45. Substitute potato mixture for croutons.)

SUGGESTED ACCOMPANIMENTS:
Ripe tomato slices
Beer

FRANKFURTERS A LA HOLSTEIN

GERMANY

For generous servings, double these amounts. Or top two frankfurters with one egg for a single serving.

4 all-beef frankfurters
  Butter
4 eggs, softly fried in butter and seasoned with
  salt and pepper

Cut frankfurters almost through, lengthwise, and open flat, butterfly fashion. Diagonally score on skin side. In a heavy frying pan over medium heat, brown well on both sides in butter. Arrange frankfurters on plates, scored side up, and top each with an egg. Makes 4 servings.

SUGGESTED ACCOMPANIMENTS:
Cabbage cole slaw
Fresh crusty rolls
Light beer

MININA
(Tunisian Terrine) TUNISIA

Minina is a dish that comes out of the Israeli section of the Tunisian cuisine. Ordinarily it is served as a first course. As a main course, it is an elegant terrinelike loaf to slice. You can eat it with a salad or serve it on buttered French bread. It is mellow enough in taste so that children can enjoy it.

¼ pound chicken livers
5 tablespoons olive oil

7 *eggs*
Salt and freshly ground black pepper
Hot-pepper sauce
1½ *cups minced cooked chicken meat*
1 *hard-cooked egg, finely diced*
¾ *cup chopped pitted green olives*
2 *teaspoons fresh lemon juice*

Simmer livers in water to cover until very tender; drain well. Put livers into a blender container, add 4 tablespoons of the olive oil, and whirl until mixture is very smooth. Beat the 7 eggs, add the liver mixture, ⅜ teaspoon salt, ¼ teaspoon pepper, and hot-pepper sauce; blend. Stir in minced chicken, hard-cooked egg, olives, and lemon juice. Taste and season generously with salt and pepper. Turn into an oiled 1-quart terrine or rectangular casserole or bread pan and spread smooth. Drip remaining oil over top. Bake in a 325° oven until mixture appears set when dish is gently shaken, about 40 to 45 minutes. Allow to cool either to warm or to room temperature. Chill if you wish. Makes 4 main-course or 6 first-course servings.

SUGGESTED ACCOMPANIMENTS:
Ripe tomato slices to garnish Minina
French bread and butter or crisp thin toast
Green lettuce salad or marinated spinach salad (seasoned with green onions, olive oil, currants, a little parsley) and lemon wedges
Light, fruity, off-dry white wine

SOUTHWEST SANDWICHES

USA

Serve these for brunch or supper. Accompany with a platter of pink and white fresh grapefruit sections, orange slices, and a garnish of feathery coriander. For the beverage, beer.

Mostly Eggs

2 *ripe avocados*
 Salt
4 *English muffins*
 Butter
8 *poached eggs*
 About 1 *cup chopped fresh coriander* (cilantro)

Peel avocados and coarsely mash with a fork with salt to season. Split, butter, and broil-toast muffins. Spread each muffin half with avocado, top with an egg, season with salt, and sprinkle with coriander. Makes 4 servings.

CHEESE-PUFF ASPARAGUS SANDWICHES
GERMANY

You pick these little sandwiches up in your hands to eat. They are excellent with a cold German Riesling.

 Cheese-Puff Diamonds (recipe below)
2 *pounds fresh asparagus, peeled, trimmed, cooked just until tender-crisp, drained well, and lightly salted*
10 *very thin slices fine smoked ham, or use prosciutto or mild coppa*

While hot, fill each diamond with part of the hot asparagus and the ham. Serve immediately. Makes 5 supper servings.

Cheese-Puff Diamonds. Combine 1 cup water, ½ cup butter, ⅜ teaspoon salt, and ¼ teaspoon ground nutmeg in a saucepan and bring to a boil. Add 1 cup sifted all-purpose flour all at once; then beat with a wooden spoon over low heat until mixture leaves sides of pan and forms a mixture that does not separate, about 1 minute. Remove from heat; continue beating to cool mixture slightly, about 2 minutes. Add 4 eggs, one at a time, and beat after each addition until mixture has a satinlike sheen. Stir in

¼ pound shredded natural sharp Gruyère or Emmenthal cheese. Spoon onto a buttered 11- by 15-inch jelly-roll pan this way: Make 2 strips, each 2 inches wide and 15 inches long and placed 4 inches apart on sheet. Bake in a 400° oven until golden, about 35 minutes. Gently cut each strip diagonally to make 5 diamonds (use ends for another purpose), and split each diamond horizontally.

NORTH CHINA STEAMED EGGS

CHINA

If you want the best Chinese food in the San Francisco area, go fifteen miles south. There, in a friendly setting, you will receive the gracious, warm welcome of elegant proprietor Eleanor Jue, and you can enjoy some spectacular and lesser-known dishes from the north of China made of exquisitely chosen, fresh ingredients. She helped me work out this recipe so that it bridges the jump from the chef in a Chinese kitchen to an American cook in a home kitchen.

You can make large individual servings: Steam 2-egg proportions in separate bowls.

For some mysterious reason, you must beat some salt with the eggs or they will not hold their fluff during steaming.

Purchase Chinese five spices in a Chinese market.

   6 *eggs*
   1 *teaspoon salt and* ⅛ *teaspoon Chinese five fragrant*
     spices or ¾ *teaspoon salt and* ¾ *teaspoon seasoned salt*
   2¼ *cups milk*
   Meat Topping (recipe below)

In a shallow heatproof soup bowl (about 1½ quarts), lightly beat eggs with salt and five spices. Add milk and beat to blend. Place bowl on steaming rack over gently boiling water in a kettle (or set bowl directly into kettle with gently boiling water 1 inch deep in bottom). Cover kettle tightly and steam until knife tip inserted in center of eggs comes out clean, about 20 minutes (remove kettle cover frequently and wipe dry of the moisture that collects inside). Gently turn meat topping over eggs. Spoon out to serve. Makes 3 to 4 servings.

Meat Topping. Cut 4 green onions with green tops into strips 1½ by ⅛ inch. Cut ½ peeled carrot into finest possible strips 1½ inches long. Mix ½ cup water, 2 tablespoons soy sauce, 2 teaspoons sugar, and 2 teaspoons cornstarch. In a heavy frying pan over high heat, quickly brown ¼ pound lean ground beef and ⅛ teaspoon salt in 1 tablespoon peanut or other salad oil. Add onions and carrots and toss just until vegetables brighten. Add cornstarch mixture and stir until it thickens slightly to sauce all ingredients.

SUGGESTED ACCOMPANIMENTS:
Steamed white rice
Fruity rosé wine

CROUTON OMELET

USA

This recipe comes from a man whose imaginative culinary mind knows no bounds or country borders. His tastes are eclectic and sure. Here he dares to put together a French omelet and croutons with Italian and Mexican seasonings.

2 *eggs*
2 *teaspoons water*
⅛ *teaspoon salt*
   Freshly ground black pepper

   2 *teaspoons butter*
   Croutons (recipe below)

Beat eggs, water, salt, and a grinding of pepper vigorously with a fork until blended. Melt butter in an 8-inch omelet pan over medium-high heat until it bubbles and begins to brown. Pour eggs into pan, and tilt pan so egg covers bottom. Lift egg edges with a thin-bladed spatula and tilt pan so uncooked egg flows to bottom of pan. When top is still creamy but barely set, spoon croutons down center. Fold top third of omelet over filling, and slip omelet out of pan onto a warm serving plate, rolling pan so that folded section falls over its extended edge. Sprinkle with cheese, parsley, and red peppers remaining in bag from crouton recipe. Makes 1 serving.

   Croutons. Trim crusts off French bread (preferably sourdough) slices, and cut into ½-inch cubes; measure ¾ cup. In a frying pan over medium heat, sauté cubes in 1½ tablespoons butter until crisp and brown. Combine 1½ to 2 tablespoons grated Parmesan cheese, 2 tablespoons finely chopped fresh parsley, and ⅛ teaspoon crushed dried red peppers in a paper bag. Add croutons and shake to coat.

   SUGGESTED ACCOMPANIMENTS:
Green salad
Beer

HELENE'S PARIS QUICHE

FRANCE

Most traditionally a first course, a quiche can be a luncheon or supper main course. Serve with a lettuce salad with an oil, vinegar, and light-mustard dressing or possibly a salad of tomato and orange slices in an oil, vinegar, and green-

onion dressing, and accompany with a chilled white table wine.

Unlike many others, this quiche calls for the pastry shell to be baked alone, then again with the filling. Do not be concerned if some of the custard slips through the crust; that creamy custard baking into the buttery shell is part of the character.

4 ounces aged natural Gruyère or Emmenthal cheese, shredded
4 ounces sliced bacon, cooked slowly until just crisp but not brown, drained, and crumbled
Baked Pastry Shell (recipe below)
3 eggs
1 cup heavy (whipping) cream
Pinch of cayenne
About ½ teaspoon ground nutmeg

Sprinkle cheese, then bacon over bottom of pastry shell. Beat eggs to blend, then beat in cream and cayenne; pour evenly over bacon. Sprinkle with nutmeg. Bake in a 325° oven until custard is set and golden, about 35 to 40 minutes. Makes 4 main-course or 8 first-course servings.

Baked Pastry Shell. Sift together into a bowl 1½ cups sifted all-purpose flour and ¼ teaspoon salt. Cut in ½ cup butter until particles are fine. Beat 1 egg with a fork, add to flour mixture, and toss to mix. Gather into a ball. Roll out on a lightly floured board to a circle to fit a 10-inch fluted French tart pan (without removable bottom) or 10-inch pie pan. Fit pastry into pan (if it tears, just press broken edges together); press dough well into sides of tart shell; make a low fluted edge on dough in pie pan. Prick well with a floured fork. Bake in a 425° oven until golden, about 15 to 18 minutes. Cool on a rack.

GOLDENROD EGGS

USA

I may never forget when my older sister came home from a ninth-grade home economics class, excited as could be about the new dish she had just learned, Eggs à la Goldenrod. She had to make the new splendor for the family immediately. She assured us that it was something on an elevated level from the usual fare around our table.

She began cooking by her mimeographed class recipe card, and my mother and father and I waited and waited and waited for supper as she labored over just how to hard-cook eggs, how to keep the lumps out of the cream sauce, what to use for sieving egg yolks, how to toast bread while doing everything else at the same time. It was all quite an undertaking.

Nevertheless, at serving time she presented us with some very pretty helpings, with a tribute to goldenrod on top of each serving: sieved egg yolks and a parsley sprig. It was good, and it still is, and it is not much work—if you have mastered hard-cooked eggs and white sauce.

This version is a little removed from the one from home ec class. It includes green onions and is served over corn bread or English muffins instead of white bread. Accompany with a siding of bacon, if desired.

¼ *cup minced green onions (white part only)*
¼ *cup butter*
3 *tablespoons all-purpose flour*
1 *teaspoon salt*
½ *teaspoon freshly ground black pepper*
3 *cups milk*
Dash of hot-pepper sauce
8 *hard-cooked eggs*
Finely chopped fresh parsley

> *Mother's Corn Bread* (recipe, page 65), *split, buttered,*
> *and crisply broil-toasted,* or *crisply toasted English*
> *muffins*

In a large, heavy saucepan, sauté onions in butter until tender.
Stir in flour, salt, and pepper to make a smooth paste. Gradually
add milk, cooking and whisking to make a smooth, slightly
thickened sauce; simmer, whisk 5 minutes. Add hot-pepper
sauce. Sieve 2 egg yolks. Chop remaining whites and eggs; add to
sauce; heat through. Ladle over corn bread. Sprinkle with
sieved yolks and parsley. Makes 4 to 6 servings.

SUGGESTED ACCOMPANIMENTS:
Bacon slices
Fresh tomatoes

SAUSAGE PIE IN PEPPER DOUGH

ITALY

The crust is thick, peppered, eggy, rich, and tender—and
more a part of the pie than a shell for it. The filling is
lightly spiced with sausages and aged cheese, and creamy
with eggs and young cheese. Wedges can be served hot at
home or at room temperature when on a picnic.

1 *package active dry yeast*
3 *tablespoons warm water*
4 *cups sifted all-purpose flour*
1½ *teaspoons salt*
1½ *teaspoons coarsely ground black pepper*
¼ *pound lard*
9 *eggs*
½ *pound fresh pork Italian garlic sausages, cut from*
   casings and crumbled

⅓ *cup chopped fresh parsley*
¾ *pound Jack cheese, shredded*
¼ *cup grated Parmesan cheese*

Sprinkle yeast into water, let soften, and stir to dissolve. Sift flour and salt together into a large mixing bowl. Stir in pepper. Cut in lard until particles are fine. Separate 1 egg; save the white. Beat the yolk with 5 whole eggs; beat in yeast mixture. Add to flour mixture and stir to make a dough. Turn out on a lightly floured board and knead until dough is soft and smooth, about 5 to 10 minutes; add no more flour than is necessary to keep dough from sticking. Turn into a greased bowl, cover, and let rise in a warm place until doubled in bulk, about 3 hours. Meantime, in a heavy frying pan over medium heat, lightly brown sausages in their own fat; stir in parsley; cool. Punch risen dough down. On a lightly floured board, roll out slightly more than half of the dough into a circle to line a heavy 9-inch frying pan; fit into pan. Sprinkle sausage over bottom and sprinkle with Jack and Parmesan cheeses. Beat remaining 3 eggs and pour evenly over sausage and cheeses. Roll out remaining dough to fit top of pie, cut with a decorative vent, place on top of filling, and flute edges to seal well. Bake in a 450° oven for 4 minutes. Reduce heat to 350° and bake for 45 minutes more. Slightly beat remaining egg white and brush over top. Bake for 15 minutes more. Cool on a rack for 10 minutes before cutting. Makes 8 servings.

SUGGESTED ACCOMPANIMENTS:
Leaf lettuce salad
Ripe tomatoes
Bright dry red table wine

Mainly Vegetable Main Courses

There is one exception to the law that says whatever is likeable is probably illegal, immoral, or fattening—vegetables. The spectacular dual virtues of vegetables are that they can taste so radiant and yet be ever so good for us. How often I wonder, when I am set before a bliss of fresh vegetables, how something so full of glow and pleasure can also be so healthy. And vegetables offer us even a third virtue: overall economy.

HOT CABBAGE-AND-POTATO SALAD

ITALY

Children's book editor Charlotte Jackson tells of her Genoese grandmother's making this dish in California in the early part of the century. Then, it was the vegetable that had to complement whatever meat they had on the menu— usually boiled beef or boiled chicken. These days, this vegetable dish could be a main supper dish, served with just a good aged Parmesan and more red wine afterward.

You must use a fine-quality olive oil. Offer red wine vinegar and more olive oil in cruets at the table for people to add according to taste.

1⅓ *pounds mature (baking) potatoes*
1 *head savoy (curly) cabbage*
About ⅔ cup olive oil
Salt and freshly ground black pepper to taste

Boil potatoes until tender, peel, and put into a chopping bowl. Meantime, wash cabbage and strip off outer dark leaves. Cut cabbage into quarters and remove core. Cook, uncovered, in a generous amount of boiling well-salted water just until tender, about 5 minutes. Time the potatoes and cabbage to be ready at about the same time. Drain cabbage well and put into bowl with potatoes. Coarsely chop together. Toss with a generous amount of oil, salt, and pepper. Serve while hot. Makes 3 main-course or 6 vegetable servings.

SUGGESTED ACCOMPANIMENT:

A bright red wine

YELLOW CROOKNECK GENOESE

ITALY

This is a sweet summer vegetable stew. Serve it in shallow soup plates and dip crusty Italian bread into the juices. Pass a bowl of freshly grated dry Jack or Parmesan to sprinkle over lightly if desired.

It conveniently works out that when the topmost squash is tender, the total dish is done.

> ¼ *pound bacon, cut into small pieces*
> 1 *large onion (preferably flat yellow or white Bermuda), thinly sliced*
> 1 *green bell pepper, finely diced*
> ⅛ *teaspoon crushed dried hot red peppers*
> 4 *ripe tomatoes, peeled, cut into wedges, and seeded*
> 1½ *pounds crookneck summer squash, cut into ⅝-inch dice*
> *Salt and freshly ground black pepper*
> *Freshly grated aged Jack or Parmesan cheese*

In a large, heavy kettle over medium heat, cook bacon until golden and soft, not crisp. Top with onion, then green pepper, red peppers, tomatoes, squash, about ½ teaspoon salt, and about ¼ teaspoon pepper. Cover and cook until squash is tender, about 30 minutes; gently shake occasionally to prevent sticking. When the squash is served, pass salt, pepper, and cheese to be added to taste. Makes about 3 main-course or 6 vegetable servings.

SUGGESTED ACCOMPANIMENTS:

Crusty Italian bread
Salad of lettuce and tender fresh spinach leaves
Very bright light dry red or full dry white wine

SPINACH STEW-SOUFFLE
(Tajine aux Epinards)   TUNISIA

In Tunisia, a tajine *is almost any baked mixture of eggs, cheese, spices, and vegetables or bits of meat or seafood. It simply must be sided with a fresh green salad. In the richer households in Tunisia, a* tajine *is usually a first course, but it can serve as a main course.*

The dish is somewhat subtle. You can taste the sweet-nesses of the onions, cheese, tomato, and spinach all coming together, boosted by the bits of hot red peppers. A good Emmenthal, sharp and sweet, is important. Pass the black-pepper grinder when you serve.

  1½ *cups finely chopped onions*
    2 *tablespoons olive oil*
    2 *tablespoons butter*
    6 *eggs*
  1½ *teaspoons tomato paste*
   ⅛ *teaspoon crushed dried hot red peppers*
   ⅛ *teaspoon freshly ground black pepper*
   ½ *cup chicken broth*
    1 *pound fresh spinach leaves (coarse stems removed before weighing), cooked until tender, well drained, and coarsely chopped*
   ½ *cup fine soft bread crumbs*
    4 *ounces natural sharp Emmenthal cheese, shredded*
     Salt

Sauté onions in oil and 1 tablespoon of the butter until limp. Beat eggs lightly with tomato paste, red peppers, black pepper, and broth. Stir in spinach, crumbs, and 3 ounces of the cheese. Taste and correct seasoning with salt, and with more black pepper if you wish. Turn into an oiled soufflé dish or similar casserole (about 2 quarts). Sprinkle with remaining cheese and dot with remaining butter. Bake in a 325° oven until mixture appears set when dish is gently shaken, about 50 to 55 minutes. Let stand for at least 10 minutes. Spoon out or cut into wedges to serve. Makes 4 servings.

SUGGESTED ACCOMPANIMENTS:
Green salad with light oil and vinegar dressing
French bread
Fresh and fruity white table wine

CAPERED CELERY ROOT IN MUSTARD SAUCE

GERMANY

Belle Rhodes is a deservedly sought-after and praised cooking teacher in the San Francisco Bay area. She was my mentor in the use of the food processor and was the source of this recipe. If you do not have a food processor, you can shred the celery root by hand. You will need about 1½ pounds of celery root as purchased to obtain 1 pound peeled.

1 *pound peeled celery root (celeriac)*
6 *tablespoons fresh lemon juice*
1 *teaspoon salt*
  Freshly ground black pepper
1 *cup heavy (whipping) cream*
2 *tablespoons Dijon-style mustard*
2 *tablespoons drained capers*
3 *to 4 tablespoons finely chopped fresh parsley*

Shred celery root or cut into pieces and pass through a food processor using the shredder plate. Immediately toss well with lemon juice, salt, and ½ teaspoon pepper. Beat cream and mustard together, pour over celery root, and mix well. Cover and chill thoroughly. At serving time, toss celery root with capers. Sprinkle with parsley. Offer additional pepper. Makes 4 main-course or 6 salad servings.

SUGGESTED ACCOMPANIMENTS:
Thin slices cold roast or boiled beef
Crusty French-style rolls
Beer

HELLENIC VEGETABLES WITH GARLIC SAUCE

GREECE

For a family that pleasures in garlic, this can be a sumptuous vegetable feast. A green salad is an essential part of the menu.

Unlike most garlic sauce thickened with bread crumbs or mashed potatoes, this one uses ground nuts.

The vegetables do not have to be absolutely hot. This is perfectly fine served at room temperature. You may find it easier to peel, slice, then cook the potatoes; but I think that the flavor is better if you cook the potatoes in their skins. If you must, you can substitute sliced canned beets for fresh ones.

2 *pounds medium-sized new potatoes*
2 *pounds trimmed beets, prepared as below*
  Salt
  Nut garlic sauce (recipe below)

Cook potatoes in boiling water until just tender, about 30 minutes; drain. When cool enough to handle, peel and cut into ¼-inch-thick slices. Arrange potato and beet slices, slightly overlapping and side by side, on warm dinner plates. Season potatoes with salt. Pass garlic sauce to spoon on top of both vegetables. Makes 4 servings.

To Prepare Fresh Beets. Scrub with vegetable brush. Leave on skin, the rootlet, and about 1 inch of the tops. Cook, covered, in boiling salted water to cover until tender, about 20 to 40 minutes. Drain, cool quickly under running water, and rub off skins under running water. Slice and serve while hot if possible.

Nut Garlic Sauce. Put in blender container 2 egg yolks, 2 tablespoons mild white wine vinegar, 1 tablespoon fresh lemon juice, 4 peeled cloves garlic, and 1 teaspoon salt; whirl to blend. With blender on low speed, gradually pour in 1 cup olive oil in a fine, steady stream through opening in container top; whirl until smooth. Stir in ½ cup ground walnuts or lightly toasted ground blanched almonds. Makes about 1¾ cups sauce.

SUGGESTED ACCOMPANIMENTS:
Leaf lettuce salad
Fresh and fruity dry white wine

BUTTER-CRUMBED ASPARAGUS EGGS
BELGIUM

It is something of a timing feat for one cook to have the asparagus hot and crisp, the crumbs golden, and the eggs mollet all done at the proper time, so a shift from mollet to hard-cooked eggs is perfectly in order if you wish.

1½ *cups fine soft French bread crumbs*
½ *cup butter*
1½ *pounds fresh asparagus, trimmed*
  4 *Eggs Mollet* (recipe below) *or* 4 *freshly cooked and finely chopped hard-cooked eggs*
    Salt
  4 *teaspoons minced fresh parsley*

    4 *teaspoons snipped fresh chives*
    Lemon wedges
    Black pepper in a grinder

In a heavy frying pan over medium heat, sauté crumbs in butter until they are crisp and deep golden and butter is slightly browned. Meantime, cook asparagus in gently boiling salted water until just tender-crisp; drain well. Arrange asparagus on two warm serving plates. Top each serving with 2 eggs mollet. Season asparagus and eggs with salt. Pour bubbling crumbs over top. Sprinkle with parsley and chives. Garnish with lemon wedges. Pass pepper grinder. Makes 2 supper servings.

    Eggs Mollet. Have 4 eggs at room temperature. In a saucepan, bring to a rapid boil enough water to cover the eggs. Place each egg on a spoon and lower it into the water. Reduce heat until water barely simmers, and cook eggs for exactly 6 minutes. Drain immediately and plunge into cold water. Peel and cut in half lengthwise.

    SUGGESTED ACCOMPANIMENT:
Fruity white table wine

GIANT EGG ROLL

USA

    •*The big egg roll-up is certainly not an authentic wrapper for Chinese Egg Roll. But when you put a crisp-vegetable egg-roll filling into it, the result is reminiscent.*

    If Chinese barbecued pork is not available to you, leave it out and increase the ham to four ounces.

    Offer two condiments, soy and hot mustard. Add soy lightly if at all. To make hot mustard, mix dry mustard with cold water to a thin paste consistency.

    2 *eggs*
    ½ *teaspoon salt*

¼ *cup sifted all-purpose flour*
½ *cup milk*
 2 *tablespoons butter*
   Crisp filling (recipe below)
 1 *green onion with green top, cut into very fine lengthwise slivers* 1½ *inches long*

Slightly beat eggs with salt. Add flour and beat until smooth. Add milk and beat again until smooth. Heat butter in a large heavy frying pan (10 to 11 inches in diameter) over medium-high heat until it bubbles. Add batter. Transfer to a 350° oven and bake for 25 minutes. With a flexible spatula, gently loosen pancake and slip onto serving platter. Spoon filling over. Roll up like a jelly roll. Sprinkle with onion. Cut crosswise into serving pieces. Serve immediately. Makes 3 to 4 servings.

Crisp filling. Shred or cut into very fine strips 1½ to 2 inches long 3 ounces cooked chicken, 2 ounces well-smoked cooked ham, and 2 ounces barbecued pork (*chahr siu*). Cut into very fine julienne strips 10 green onions with green tops, 3 ounces Chinese edible-pod (sugar) peas with ends and strings removed, and 2 ounces canned or fresh bamboo shoots. Have ready 3 ounces bean sprouts. Heat 3 tablespoons peanut or other salad oil over high heat in a large heavy frying pan. Add ham and onions and toss to coat with oil. Add remaining ingredients and lightly stir and cook just until barely wilted, about 2 to 3 minutes. Remove from heat and generously season to taste with salt (about ¾ teaspoon) and freshly ground white pepper (about ½ teaspoon).

SPINACH PIE
(Spanakopita) GREECE

Spanakopita *can do no wrong in my book. It provides blissful contemplation of butter-beaded thin layers of fine filo to light golden crisp around a filling of favorite tastes.*

It is worth spending the few cents more for imported feta. It is usually tangier and more flavorful than domestic.

Once you begin, be sure to keep filo sheets enclosed in plastic or covered with a damp towel until ready to use in order to prevent drying.

1½ *pounds fresh spinach leaves (stems removed before*
    weighing) or about 2½ *cups chopped cooked spinach*
1 *cup finely chopped onions*
⅓ *cup minced green onions with part of green tops*
½ *cup olive oil*
¼ *cup finely chopped fresh parsley*
¼ *cup finely chopped fresh dill leaves or about* 2½
    teaspoons crumbled dried dillweed
    Salt and freshly ground black pepper
4 *eggs*
⅓ *cup milk*
½ *pound imported feta cheese, crumbled*
½ *cup pine nuts*
1 *cup melted butter*
9 *sheets (each about* 18 *by* 12 *inches) prepared filo (phyllo)*

Wash and drain spinach. Cook, covered, in water that clings to the leaves just until tender. Drain, chop finely, and drain again very well. Sauté chopped onions and green onions in olive oil until soft and transparent. Add parsley, dill, ½ teaspoon salt, and ¼ teaspoon pepper, and sauté for a few moments more. Lightly beat eggs and beat in milk. Stir in spinach, onion mixture, feta, and pine nuts. Taste and correct seasoning with salt and pepper. Brush a 9-inch pie pan (1½ inches deep) with melted butter. Brush 1 sheet of filo generously with butter and arrange in the pan to line it, letting excess filo hang over pan sides. Repeat with 4 more sheets, shifting the lengthwise direction of each sheet so that the long filo overhangs are arranged around pan. Turn in spinach mixture and spread smooth. Cut 4 more filo sheets to fit top of pie plate. Brush each with butter, and place over spinach. Fold over bottom sheets to enclose and seal the pie, brushing well with butter. Bake in a 350° oven until golden, about 50 minutes. Cool on a rack slightly before serving, or serve at room temperature. Cut into wedges with a serrated knife. Makes 6 main-course or 10 first-course servings.

SUGGESTED ACCOMPANIMENTS:
Ripe tomatoes garnished with black olives
Fresh and flavorful dry white wine
Grapes and/or melon

POTATOES IN SLEEPING ROBES
(Kartoffel im Schlafrock)   AUSTRIA

A friend of mine used to help with autumn field work at his cousin's place when he was a boy in the high Tyrol. The girls of the family would bring the noonday meal to the workers in the fields. It consisted of potatoes just dug from the earth, boiled in their skins, and still warm; coarse salt; whole caraway seeds; a mound of fresh unsalted butter; local cheeses; and cold, freshly churned buttermilk. Each worker would take a potato, peel it, dip it into salt and caraway seeds, scoop off some butter and pack it onto the potato, add a cut of cheese, and bite into it. Then he would drink buttermilk.

The same eating event took place back at his home in

Innsbruck. There the traditional way to serve the potatoes (somewhat to the consternation of the women who had to do the laundry) was to spread out a clean white linen table-cloth on the dining table, mound the hot potatoes right on the cloth, and progress as above, but with the aid of individual plates and silverware.

To carry off the luscious custom here, I bow to our own habits by putting the potatoes on a platter and letting each diner work on his own little feast from his own plate. I offer beer as well as buttermilk, and I add a big butter-lettuce salad at the end.

There is no recipe. Just boil plenty of scrubbed small new potatoes in their skins, offer about three cheeses of your choice (all with rather direct and uncomplicated flavors, such as a Swiss, Muenster, and Jack or Teleme), have available lots of fresh sweet butter, caraway seeds, and coarse salt.

Should you have the slightest qualm about the nutritional sufficiency of this meal, a report from the Agricultural Research Service of the United States Department of Agriculture states: "A diet of whole milk and potatoes would supply almost all the food elements necessary for the maintenance of the human body." And there is this potato praise from Dr. Paul Lachance, professor of nutritional physiology at Rutgers University: "Potatoes are one high-nutrition food. They are not a starch but a low-calorie, high-water-content (80%) food, with all of the essential amino acids of good-quality protein, three B vitamins, iron, and the second-best source of Vitamin C we know. Potatoes contain less than one percent fat. Ounce for ounce, they are not more fattening than an ordinary apple."

Giant Egg Rolls [IRWIN HOROWITZ]

Fillets in Dill Sauce served with new potatoes, buttered green beans and ripe tomatoes. [IRWIN HOROWITZ]

Caribbean Coconut Chicken—shown here with corn bread, a pear-lettuce salad and orange sherbet sprinkled with dark chocolate. [IRWIN HOROWITZ]

Individual Pot Roasts with Cheese-Crumb Pasta served wth tossed salad, fresh orange slices and corn bread patties. [WOMAN'S DAY STUDIOS]

Beef and Onion Stew II [ROBERT COATES]

Apple Pancake Pie (right)—shown here with other delicious apple desserts.
[IRWIN HOROWITZ]

Oven-roasted Sweet Cheesecakes [ROBERT COATES]

Barb's Blueberry Tart—shown here with a variation of the recipe using strawberries and eliminating the sour cream. [ROBERT COATES]

Fresh and Dry Beans

Beans of all kinds seem to will pork to accompany them—
in the cooking or in the eating. The reasons are sound and
several: sumptuous taste, counterpoint textures, completing
nutrition. The recipes in this chapter celebrate the satisfy-
ing pairing.

ITALIAN BEANS AND POTATOES

ITALY

It is important to add the beans to the pan before the potatoes so the beans can take up their share of the seasonings ahead of the more absorbent potatoes.

1 *pound whole Italian (Romano) green beans, rinsed*
and ends trimmed
1¼ *pounds unpeeled small new potatoes, scrubbed*
¼ *to* ⅓ *pound salt pork with rind and salt edge trimmed,*
finely ground
⅓ *cup olive oil*
4 *large pressed cloves garlic*
Freshly ground black pepper
Salt

Separately, in boiling salted water, cook beans, uncovered, and potatoes, covered, until just tender; drain well. In a large, heavy frying pan over medium heat, brown pork well in oil. Stir in garlic, then beans. Add potatoes. Sauté, gently turning, until vegetables are heated through. Season with pepper, and with salt if necessary. Makes 3 supper servings.

SUGGESTED ACCOMPANIMENTS:
Abundant garden-fresh tomatoes
Bright dry red wine, as a California Grignolino or Italian Chianti

BEANS AND HAM AND CORN BREAD

USA

So far as I know, this is strictly American. It used to be the response to a cold winter's day at our house when I was growing up.

Fresh and Dry Beans

A German version, I am told, is to put the beans and ham over spaetzle instead of corn bread. Coleslaw should taste good with either version.

> 2 *cups small dry white beans (Great Northerns or*
> *navy), rinsed*
> *About 7 cups water*
> 1½ *pounds meaty smoked ham hocks, sawed into several*
> *pieces (trim out any excess fat if you wish)*
> *Freshly ground black pepper*
> *Salt*
> *Mother's Corn Bread* (recipe below)

Put beans, water, and ham into a large kettle. Cover and cook over low heat until beans are tender and ham falls off bone easily, about 3 to 4 hours. Remove bones. Add pepper to taste and salt if necessary. For each serving, split a corn-bread square, put halves into a soup plate, and ladle ham and beans over. Makes 4 to 6 servings.

Mother's Corn Bread. Beat 2 eggs in a mixing bowl. Beat in 1 cup milk, 6 tablespoons melted butter, and 1 cup yellow corn-meal. Sift together into the bowl 1 cup sifted all-purpose flour, 2 tablespoons sugar, 4 teaspoons baking powder, and 1 teaspoon salt. Stir just until blended. Turn into a buttered 9-inch-square baking pan. Bake in a 400° oven until deep golden, about 25 minutes. Cut into squares.

SUGGESTED ACCOMPANIMENTS:
More corn bread, buttered
Cole slaw
Dry red wine

GLORIA SAUSAGES WITH BEANS AND BASIL

ITALY

This dish is an institution at my table at least once during midsummer when the fresh basil and the Italian beans are both prime. It makes an excellent supper, with good Italian bread and ripe fresh tomatoes and a light and dry California Zinfandel. Fresh corn is fine with it too.

The idea comes from Alda, of Piedmontese descent. Gloria is the brand of quality sausages made by her family in San Francisco's North Beach.

⅔ *pound fresh pork large-link Italian sausages (mildly spiced, with garlic)*
1 *pound fresh Italian (Romano) green beans or regular green beans, trimmed and cut into 2-inch diagonal lengths*
2 *tablespoons butter*
1 *tablespoon dry white table wine*
2 *to 3 large pressed cloves garlic*
Salt and freshly ground black pepper to taste
⅓ *to ½ cup finely chopped fresh basil leaves*

Put cold water to ⅛-inch depth in a large, heavy frying pan. Add sausages, cover tightly, and simmer for 15 minutes, turning once. Remove and save all except ⅓ cup of the liquid in pan. Cook sausages over medium heat, uncovered, until they brown well on all sides and cook for 15 minutes; add a little reserved liquid to pan as necessary. Meantime, cook beans, uncovered, in boiling salted water until tender-crisp; drain well. Remove any drippings in pan in excess of 2 tablespoons. Slice sausages diagonally into 1½-inch pieces. Add butter, wine, garlic, beans, salt, and pepper. Sauté, turning, until beans are heated through and flavors are blended. Sprinkle with basil. Makes 2 supper servings.

SAUSAGE WITH LIMAS
(Coteghino) ITALY

A proper coteghino should contain some ground pork rind and be wonderfully meaty and juicy. It should also be gently but deeply spiced. A number of Italian sausage makers make good coteghinos, and those plump giant link sausages are worth seeking.

2 *cups large dry lima beans, rinsed*
1 *whole coteghino (1 to 1½ pounds)*
1 *large onion, thinly sliced*
2 *tablespoons butter*
   Salt and freshly ground black pepper
2 *large sprigs fresh sage or ½ teaspoon ground sage*

Put beans into a kettle with 5 cups cold water, heat to boiling, boil for 2 minutes, remove from heat, cover, and let stand for 1 hour. Cover and simmer until beans are just tender, about 45 minutes. In another kettle, cover coteghino with water; cover and simmer for 45 minutes. Remove casing from sausage and cut sausage into ⅜-inch-thick slices. Sauté onions in butter until tender, and add to beans along with 1 teaspoon salt, ⅛ teaspoon pepper, and the sage. Tuck sausage slices among beans. (Add a little more water if necessary in order to have a juicy dish.) Cover and bake in a 350° oven for about 30 minutes. Correct seasoning with a generous amount of salt and pepper. Makes 6 servings.

SUGGESTED ACCOMPANIMENTS:
Bread sticks
Fresh leaf spinach or chard
Red wine

RUM BLACK BEANS

CUBA

If you cannot find black beans in your supermarket, you can buy them (also called turtle beans) in health-food stores and Mexican, Spanish, and Chinese food markets.
Rice is imperative with this dish.

   1 *pound dried black beans, picked over, washed, and drained*
   6 *cups cold water*
   2 *pounds meaty smoked ham hocks, sawed into 1-inch pieces (trim out any excess fat)*
1½ *cups chopped onions*
   1 *medium-sized green bell pepper, chopped*
   2 *large pressed cloves garlic*
  ½ *cup olive oil*
   1 *large bay leaf*
   1 *teaspoon* each *crumbled dried thyme and oregano*
  ⅛ *teaspoon crushed dried hot red peppers*
    Salt
    Freshly ground black pepper
  ⅓ *cup dark Jamaica rum*
   2 *cups commercial sour cream at room temperature*

Put beans, water, and ham into a large kettle. Heat to boiling, boil for 2 minutes, remove from heat, cover, and let stand for 1 hour. In a large frying pan, sauté onions, green pepper, and garlic in oil until limp. Add to beans along with bay leaf, thyme, oregano, red peppers, 1 teaspoon salt, and ¼ teaspoon black pepper. Cover and simmer until beans are tender, about 2 hours. Remove ham bones. Stir in ¼ cup of the rum. Bake, uncovered, in a 350° oven for 30 minutes. Stir in remaining rum. Correct seasoning with salt and pepper. Pass sour cream to top each serving. Makes 6 servings.

Fresh and Dry Beans

SUGGESTED ACCOMPANIMENTS:
Hot white rice
Dry rosé wine
Orange-banana-coconut ambrosia

BOMISCH BEANS

CZECHOSLOVAKIA

Bömisch *refers to the cooking style in the western part of old Czechoslovakia.*

Make the beans the main item for supper, and side with a cold platter of rather mildly smoked German-type sausages such as Thuringer and mettwurst, thinly sliced, with a little mustard, good bread, and cold beer.

2½ *cups fine soft crumbs from French-style bread*
    (preferably sourdough)
1 *cup butter*
1½ *pounds fresh Italian (Romano) beans*
    Salt
    Lemon wedges

In a large, heavy frying pan over medium heat, sauté crumbs in butter until they are crisp and deep golden and butter is slightly browned. Meantime, cook beans, uncovered, in boiling well-salted water until tender. Drain well. Season generously with salt and turn onto serving plates. Spoon crumbs and butter over. Garnish with lemon wedges, and squeeze on juice to taste as you eat. Makes 4 supper servings.

SUPPER STEW FOCSANI

YUGOSLAVIA

"When I make this, we eat ourselves crazy," says the mother who told me about this Serbian dish. You cook the ham-rich beans and the sauerkraut separately, but you have to overlap the beans and sauerkraut as you eat in order to get their special flavors.

2 cups (1 pound) dry cranberry beans, rinsed
7 cups cold water
   About 2½ pounds meaty smoked ham hocks, sawed into
   several pieces (trim out any excess fat)
1½ cups finely chopped onions
3 tablespoons olive oil
1 large can (1 pound, 11 ounces) sauerkraut, rinsed and
   drained well
   Freshly ground black pepper
   Salt

Put beans, water, and ham into a large kettle. Heat to boiling. Boil for 2 minutes, remove from heat, cover, and let stand for 1 hour. Simmer, covered, until beans and meat are tender, about 1½ hours. Remove ham bones. In a large frying pan, sauté onions in oil until tender. Add sauerkraut, ½ teaspoon pepper, and about 1 cup of the liquid from beans. Cover and simmer, stirring occasionally, for 20 to 30 minutes. Season both beans and sauerkraut generously with salt and very generously with pepper. Serve side by side in warm rimmed dinner plates. Makes 6 servings.

SUGGESTED ACCOMPANIMENTS:
Whole or mashed boiled new potatoes
Lettuce salad (optional)
Light and fruity dry red wine or beer

MR. MANETTA'S BUTTER BEANS AND SAUSAGES

GREECE

When I visited Athens some years ago, Mr. Manetta kindly took time out from his rush of duties to explain his theory of why Greek food is so successfully seasoned, and he gave me the recipe for his own cooking specialty. The best Greek cooks, he said, treat each major part of a dish separately, then combine it with other parts; they do not season the combined ingredients all at once.

1 *pound fresh pork Italian garlic sausages (preferably seasoned with fennel)*
Olive oil
2 *cups finely chopped onions*
3 *large pressed cloves garlic*
1 *can (1 pound) peeled whole tomatoes, broken up*
1 *can (8 ounces) tomato sauce*
½ *teaspoon sugar*
1½ *teaspoons salt*
¾ *teaspoon freshly ground black pepper*
Cooked Limas (recipe below)
¾ *cup chopped fresh parsley*

In an oiled large, heavy frying pan, bake sausages in a 350° oven, turning once, until lightly browned, 20 to 30 minutes. Remove and cut into 2-inch diagonal slices. Add enough oil to frying pan to make 3 tablespoons. Add onions and sauté until limp. Stir in remaining ingredients except ¼ cup of the parsley. Cover and simmer for about 45 minutes, stirring occasionally. Sprinkle with remaining parsley. Makes 4 to 5 servings.

Cooked Limas. Put 1½ cups large dry lima beans, rinsed, into a large kettle. Add enough cold water to cover deeply. Heat to boiling; boil for 2 minutes; remove from heat, cover, and let stand for 1 hour. Drain, rinse, and cover with fresh salted water. Heat to boiling, then gently boil, uncovered, until beans are tender, about 45 minutes; drain.

SUGGESTED ACCOMPANIMENTS:

Cooked chard dressed with oil, vinegar, salt, and pepper served
   at room temperature
Large bread sticks or crusty bread
Full fruity red table wine, as a hearty California Zinfandel
Chilled fresh orange segments

A TYROLEAN SUPPER

AUSTRIA

The Tyrolean who told me of this dish insists that the only way to get the full flavor and pleasure is to mash the potatoes into the sauce as you eat. He recommends beer with it, also crisp radishes and perhaps a compote of cinnamon-spiced apples for dessert.

When it is available, smoked shoulder butt may replace the ham hocks, with these recipe changes: Use a 2-pound lean boneless smoked shoulder butt. Simmer it for about 1½ hours. Carve at serving time.

   3 pounds meaty ham hocks, sawed into 1-inch-thick
     pieces (trim out any excess fat)
   3 cups finely chopped onions
   6 tablespoons melted fat trimmings from the ham or
     salad oil or lard
   ¼ cup flour
   1 teaspoon ground nutmeg
   ½ teaspoon salt
   ½ teaspoon freshly ground black pepper

½ teaspoon crumbled dried basil

4 pressed cloves garlic

1½ pounds potatoes, peeled and cut into 1-inch-thick
   crosswise slices

1 pound fresh green beans, cut in half crosswise and
   ends trimmed

Dijon-style mustard

Put ham into a kettle with water just to cover. Cover and simmer for 1 hour. In a heavy, large kettle over medium heat, sauté onions in fat until tender and browned. Sprinkle with flour and stir. Gradually stir in 2½ cups of the broth from cooking meat (pour off remaining broth). Add nutmeg, salt, pepper, basil, and garlic. Cook, stirring, for a few minutes until blended and slightly thickened. Arrange cooked ham in center of kettle; put potatoes on one side of ham and beans on the other. Cover tightly and simmer until potatoes and beans are very tender, about 1½ hours; gently turn meat and vegetables once or twice. At serving time, arrange ham in center of warm serving platter and arrange potatoes and beans on either side. Taste sauce, correct seasoning, and pour over. Offer mustard. Makes 4 to 6 servings.

Corn in Seven Aspects

Wherever corn grows in the world, it achieves great popularity. It is not an obscure part of a cuisine; it is obvious, nearly a mainstay—as fresh kernels in Colombia and Peru, hominy and masa in Mexico, polenta in Italy, sweet corn, hominy, and cornmeal in the United States. Even French cooks went wild for it when they finally took a fair look at sweet corn as something different from "horse corn."

No wonder. Corn, in nearly all its forms—sweet, dried, whole, ground, pulverized, burst—gives a taste that must be among the most satisfying of any in the world. There is nothing nebulous about that flavor; it is solid, but nature never lets it be too bold or jarring. Tasting corn gives you plenty to think about because you can find so many complexities and subtleties behind the first pleasing sweet savoriness. And this is not to mention corn textures, which are just as compelling.

Of all the starches, cornmeal may be among the most cordial; it takes up and takes to so many other ingredients so genially.

SANTA FEREÑO EGGS

In earlier times, Bogotá was called Santa Fe. So the customs of the citizens carry the Santa Fereño appellation. One of the most enchanting of those customs is called simply Santa Fereño. It is a sort of four o'clock high tea, but with a divine difference. The menu:

Eggs Softly Scrambled—with fresh corn kernels

Butter-Sautéed Ripe Plantain Slices

Hot Colombian Chocolate with Cheese—full chocolate flavor, frothy-topped, with mellow cheese broken into it, warmed, and spooned out, sweet and slightly softened

Fresh Buns—chewy, of yucca flour, four o'clock-fresh from a nearby bakery oven

Sugar Cookies and Shortbreads—optional

I do not keep the custom for high teatime. I move it to a supper or late-supper position and adapt it for us a little further: Make portions ample for a main meal. Substitute bananas for plantains. Make my best hot chocolate and beat it to frothiness. Use young Jack cheese for melting or dunking (perfectly courteous in this context). Use local fresh yeast buns, preferably open-celled, moist, chewy, and egg-glazed.

4 tablespoons butter
Kernels cut from 3 or 4 ears fresh corn
½ teaspoon sugar
Salt
8 eggs
2 tablespoons cream or milk
Freshly ground black pepper
Fried Bananas (recipe below)

Melt butter in a large, heavy frying pan over medium heat. Add corn, sugar, and ¼ teaspoon salt, and sauté until corn is tender, about 3 minutes. Beat eggs with cream, ¼ teaspoon salt, and a grinding of pepper. Add to pan and softly scramble, keeping eggs very moist. Serve immediately, bordered with fried bananas. Makes 4 servings.

Fried Bananas. Peel 4 ripe but firm bananas and cut in half lengthwise. In a frying pan, heat 3 to 4 tablespoons butter over medium heat until it bubbles. Add bananas and sauté on both sides just until heated through.

FRESH CORN IN SOUR CREAM

USA

There is an easy temptation to add more bacon to this recipe. But resist it. A little is just right for this seasoning. Add more sugar if the corn is not especially fresh out of the field.

> 2 *ounces sliced bacon*
> 6 *ears corn, husks and silks removed*
> 6 *tablespoons minced green onions with part of green tops*
> 3 *tablespoons butter*
> 1⅓ *cups commercial sour cream*
> 1 *teaspoon salt*
> ½ *teaspoon freshly ground black pepper*
> ¼ *teaspoon sugar*
> ⅛ *teaspoon ground nutmeg*
> 1½ *teaspoons finely chopped fresh parsley*

Slowly cook bacon until crisp, drain on paper towels, and crumble. Place corn in a large kettle with cold water to cover. Heat to just boiling; remove corn, drain, and cut kernels off cob. Meantime, in a large, heavy frying pan, sauté onions in butter until limp. Reduce heat to low. Stir in sour cream, salt, pepper, sugar, and nutmeg. Fold in corn and half of the bacon and just heat through. Sprinkle with remaining bacon and with parsley. Makes 2 or 3 main-course or 4 to 6 vegetable servings.

SUGGESTED ACCOMPANIMENTS:

Sliced ripe tomatoes
Lettuce salad
Buttered toast strips
Fruity white table wine, as a California Johannisberg Riesling

CHAN'S CORN AND PORK

CHINA

Chan Wong explains that ordinarily, in a Cantonese meal, this dish would be only one of several served as the main part of the meal. But it can be a main dish alone when made with a generous proportion of pork to corn and when sided with steamed rice and a green vegetable such as spinach.

He explains further that the reason for the cornstarch is that the thickening effect will pick up all the flavorful juices in the sauté and hold them in.

He suggests that you offer a choice of condiments: Chinese hoi sin *sauce (slightly sweet bean sauce) and Japanese* shichimi togarashi *(see explanation, pages 103–104).*

This dish works best in a big wok. In whatever vessel you use, do not crowd pork in pan as you brown it; if necessary, brown only half at a time. Cook the dish quickly.

¼ *cup chicken broth*
¼ *cup dry sherry*
2 *tablespoons brown sugar*
4 *teaspoons soy sauce*

1 *teaspoon salt*

1½ *tablespoons cornstarch*

¾ *pound boneless pork shoulder, cut into strips* 1½ *by* ⅛ *inch*

3 *tablespoons peanut* or *other salad oil*

1 *can (12 ounces) whole-kernel white corn, drained*

9 *or* 10 *green onions with green tops, slit lengthwise and cut into* 1½-*inch lengths*

Mix broth with sherry, 1 tablespoon of the sugar, 3 teaspoons of the soy sauce, ½ teaspoon of the salt, and ½ tablespoon of the cornstarch. Toss pork with remaining 1 tablespoon sugar, 1 teaspoon soy sauce, ½ teaspoon salt, and 1 tablespoon cornstarch, and with 1 tablespoon of the oil. Heat remaining 2 tablespoons oil in a wok or large, heavy frying pan over high heat. When very hot, add pork and toss until browned. Remove with a slotted spoon. Add corn to pan and sauté to coat with drippings. Stir in onions. Add broth mixture and stir to coat all ingredients. Return pork to pan and turn to heat through. Makes 4 servings.

SUGGESTED ACCOMPANIMENT:
Fruity rosé wine

BAKED MAIZE OF ROMANIA
(Mamaliga)   **ROMANIA**

We do not hear much about Romanian mamaliga, *probably because it is the staple for peasants and others who do hard physical labor, and the simple foods of a land are usually not touted and broadcast so much as the more aristocratic ones.*

Mamaliga, a coarsely ground cornmeal, is the staple special to Romania in the way that rice is to China, beans are to South America, potatoes are to northern Europe, and pasta is to Italy. It has many uses in Romania—as morning porridge; as polenta, topped with kidneys or game or mushrooms or sweetbreads in sauce; or sliced and fried in butter with a softly fried egg; or with sour cream, fresh sheep's milk cheese, and poached eggs.

3½ cups water
  1 teaspoon salt
  1 cup polenta
  1 cup commercial sour cream
1½ ounces feta cheese (preferably imported from Romania
    or Bulgaria), crumbled
  3 tablespoons butter
  4 poached eggs
    Black pepper in a grinder

In a heavy kettle, heat water and salt to boiling. Stirring constantly with a wooden spoon, gradually add polenta. Gently boil, stirring, for about 3 minutes. Then cook over low heat, stirring frequently, until mixture is thick, about 25 minutes. Turn into a buttered shallow casserole, about 1 quart. Spread sour cream over top, sprinkle with feta, and dot with butter. Broil about 8 inches from heat until golden. Arrange poached eggs on top. Cut and lift out each serving. Pass black pepper. Makes 4 servings.

SUGGESTED ACCOMPANIMENTS:
Cooked leaf spinach
Dry rosé wine

PINE NUT POLENTA
(Pignoli Polenta)   ITALY

You can compile this dish a few hours ahead and bake it just in time to serve. It is complete as a supper dish, but I like to side it with roasted Italian garlic pork sausages (spiced with fennel, if possible): Put 1½ to 2 pounds sausages in a buttered shallow pan and bake in a 350° oven for 30 minutes, basting occasionally with butter. Slice diagonally.

1¾ *cups finely chopped onions*
½ *cup butter*
  1 *cup polenta or yellow cornmeal*
  4 *cups water*
  1 *teaspoon salt*
  1 *pound Teleme or Jack cheese, cut into ¼-inch thick*
    slices
½ *cup toasted pine nuts*
¼ *cup golden raisins*
  2 *tablespoons grated Parmesan cheese*

Sauté onions in half of the butter until limp. Stir together polenta and 2 cups cold water. In a large saucepan, heat the remaining 2 cups water with the salt to boiling; add cornmeal mixture. Cook, whisking, until mixture comes to a full boil. Then cook over medium heat, whisking, for 5 minutes. Stir in onions. Spread half of the polenta mixture over bottom of a buttered shallow 2-quart baking dish. Top with half of the Teleme, half of the pine nuts, and all of the raisins. Top with remaining polenta, remaining Teleme, and remaining pine nuts. Melt remaining butter and pour over to cover surface. Sprinkle with Parmesan. Bake in a 350° oven for 50 minutes. Spoon out to serve. Makes 6 servings.

SUGGESTED ACCOMPANIMENTS:
Fresh spinach salad
Bright red wine, as a dry California Grignolino or a Chianti
Fresh peaches or oranges

MUSHROOM-MEAT SAUCE
WITH CHEESE POLENTA

ITALY

This meat sauce is also fine over plain boiled polenta or narrowly stripped pasta.

If you are serving only six, cut down the following polenta proportions by one-fourth.

½ *pound bulk pork sausage*
1 *pound ground beef round*
3 *cups finely chopped onions*
3 *large pressed cloves garlic*
½ *cup finely chopped fresh parsley*
½ *pound fresh mushrooms, thinly sliced*
3 *cans (8 ounces each) tomato sauce*
2 *cups dry red table wine*
1 *teaspoon salt*
½ *teaspoon ground sage*
¼ *teaspoon each crumbled dried rosemary, marjoram, thyme, and freshly ground black pepper*
Cheese Polenta (recipe below)

In a large heavy kettle over medium heat, brown sausage until crumbly; add round and brown. Add onions and sauté until limp. Stir in garlic, parsley, and mushrooms; then stir in remaining ingredients except polenta. Cover loosely and slowly simmer, stirring occasionally, until reduced to thick sauce consistency, about 2½ hours. Makes 6 to 8 servings.

Cheese Polenta. In a large kettle, heat 6 cups water and 2 teaspoons salt to boiling. Stirring constantly with a wire whisk, gradually add 1¾ cups polenta or yellow cornmeal. Gently boil, whisking, for 5 minutes. Turn into an oiled shallow baking dish, about 2 quarts, and top with 1 pound Teleme or Jack cheese, cut into small chunks. Bake in a 350° oven until set, about 40 minutes.

SUGGESTED ACCOMPANIMENTS:
Green salad
Italian bread sticks
Dry red wine

RIBBON CASCADES
WITH SESAME CORNMEAL

YUGOSLAVIA

This recipe provides an excellent use of leftover boiled smoked tongue or any well-smoked ham.

½ *cup butter*
¼ *cup fresh lemon juice*
1 *teaspoon salt*
2 *pressed cloves garlic*
1 *eggplant (about 1 pound), peeled and cut into julienne strips*
10 *green onions with part of green tops, cut into julienne strips*
¾ *pound summer squash (unpeeled patty pan or peeled zucchini), cut into julienne strips*
2 *small stalks celery, cut into julienne strips*
1 *green bell pepper, cut into julienne strips*
1 *pound cooked smoked tongue or well-smoked ham, cut into julienne strips*
Sesame Cornmeal (recipe below)
Finely chopped fresh parsley
Lemon wedges
Black pepper in a grinder

Melt butter in a very large frying pan and stir in lemon juice, salt, and garlic. Add eggplant, onions, squash, celery, green pepper, and tongue. Sauté over medium-high heat until vegetables are just tender, about 10 minutes. Add salt if necessary. To serve: Spoon out cornmeal and side with vegetables and juices. Sprinkle lightly with parsley, garnish with lemon wedges, and pass black pepper. Makes 6 servings.

Sesame Cornmeal. In a large kettle, heat 5 cups water and 1½ teaspoons salt to boiling. Stirring constantly with a wire whisk, gradually add 1¼ cups polenta or yellow cornmeal. Gently boil, whisking, for 5 minutes. Turn into a buttered shallow baking dish, about 1½ quarts. Pour 5 tablespoons melted butter evenly over. Sprinkle with 4 tablespoons lightly toasted sesame seeds. Bake in a 350° oven until set, about 40 minutes.

NOTE: Cut all the julienne strips about 2 inches long and ⅛ inch wide.

SUGGESTED ACCOMPANIMENTS:
Sautéed fresh spinach
Dry rosé wine

Other Grains

They do not just carry flavors. They take them into them-selves. That is a unique and wonderful thing about grains.

It is why they offer just about as much chance for a great rush of taste as anything you can cook. It is part of why they are so economical: They load you with taste satisfaction. The other part is that they are simply nutritious and give a sense of volume satisfaction.

Other vehicles for sauces and enclosing juices, such as pastes and cornmeal and potatoes, hold onto their identities in the midst of succulent surroundings. But the subjects of this chapter are willing to give themselves up and absorb whatever is nice swirling about them.

The difference between keeping and letting go of identity seems to have held through the ages as cooking standards were set. We mark a lovely paste dish by the fact that the paste does not get subjugated to the sauce. Potato salad may be a grand mingling of chosen flavors; but to be right, it has to bear the clear taste and texture of potatoes. And if you do not recognize that you have encountered milled corn when you dip into a polenta dish, you have missed a main point of polenta.

But what do we worry in a lentil-and-sausage stew if the lentils shed some of their shape and just offer up their heady background taste? What would be the use of a risotto if each of those crunchy rice grains tasted purely of rice and not of rice with its ultimate intake of mushroom broth and butter and onions and wine? And don't we mostly love barley for the soup it sets in, and the stew it thickens, and the tastes it takes up as it simmers in broth to a pilaf— rather than barley for itself alone?

Knowing this absorptive trait of grains behooves a cook to champion it. You have to season amply, enough for whatever surrounds the grain plus enough to allow for the fact that the grain is going to steal about half of that surrounding seasoning for itself—obviously in a beneficent way.

LENTIL-AND-RICE PILAF
(Rizza, Dlokhi) IRAN

In his restaurant, Narsai extends his Continental menu with exotic Assyrian delights from the recipe heritage of his own family. One of these is Rizza, Dlokhi, *a pilaf of buttered rice, lentils, and onions bejeweled with dried apricots. It is a gentle glory topped with any fine yogurt, but a thing even more supreme when gilded with Cousin Sam's homemade yogurt. That edible white velvet is so rich that you would think it was sour cream. Yet it is so refreshing and tangy that you know that it has to be the best possible yogurt.*

Such a pilaf with such a topping makes a luxuriously wholesome main dish, even though Narsai usually serves it as an accompaniment to barbecued or roast leg of lamb.

> ¾ *cup lentils, rinsed*
> *Salt*
> 1¼ *cups finely chopped onions*
> 9 *tablespoons butter*
> ¾ *cup (about 4 ounces) moist dried apricots, coarsely cut up*
> 2 *cups long-grain white rice, cooked until barely tender, rinsed, and drained*
> *Parsley sprigs*
> *At least 2 cups plain yogurt at room temperature*

Simmer lentils, covered, in salted water to cover generously until tender, about 30 minutes; drain; add salt to taste. In a heavy frying pan over medium heat, sauté onions in 3 tablespoons of the butter until transparent. Stir in apricots and about ⅜ tea-spoon salt and heat through. Salt rice to taste, and spread one-third of it over bottom of a 2½-quart buttered shallow baking dish. Spoon onions and apricots evenly over. Top with one-third more of the rice, the lentils, then remaining rice. Dot with remaining 6 tablespoons butter. Cover and bake in a 350° oven until heated through, about 30 minutes. Garnish with parsley sprigs. Pass yogurt to spoon over top. Makes 5 or 6 main-course or 8 accompaniment servings.

SUGGESTED ACCOMPANIMENTS:
Fresh leaf spinach salad
Dry white or light dry rosé wine

BARRANQUILLA COCONUT RICE
COLOMBIA

On the Caribbean coast of Colombia, the fruit border would be fried plantains rather than fried bananas.

If you wish, you can accompany this rice with small cube or minute steaks browned in butter and well seasoned with salt and pepper. In that case, serve the egg on top of the steak instead of the rice.

   Butter
4 *pressed cloves garlic*
3 *tablespoons fresh lemon juice*
2 *cups flaked coconut*
¾ *cup moist seedless raisins*
2 *cups long-grain white rice, cooked just until tender, rinsed, and drained*
   Salt and freshly ground black pepper
   Fried Bananas (recipe, page 76, except *use 3 bananas and about 3 tablespoons butter*)
6 *or* 12 *eggs, softly fried in butter and seasoned with salt and pepper*

Heat ½ cup butter in a large frying pan until it foams and begins to brown. Remove from heat and stir in garlic, lemon juice, coconut, and raisins. Thoroughly mix in rice. Season generously with salt (at least 1 teaspoon) and pepper (at least ½ teaspoon). Turn into a buttered shallow baking-serving dish, about 2 quarts. Cover and bake in a 350° oven until heated through, about 30 minutes. Serve each person rice topped with one or two eggs and a banana slice alongside. Makes 6 servings.

SUGGESTED ACCOMPANIMENT:
Light beer

RISOTTO AFTER JAMES BEARD AND HAROLYN THOMPSON

ITALY

Total cooking time for this dish will be in the neighborhood of twenty to thirty minutes. The grains of rice will be soft and creamy, yet separate.

½ *ounce imported Italian dried mushrooms, broken into small bits*
½ *cup water*
½ *cup dry white table wine*
¼ *cup minced onions*
  9 *tablespoons butter*
  1 *cup long-grain white rice* or *short-grain pearl rice*
    About 3 cups hot homemade chicken broth
    Freshly grated Parmesan cheese
    Hot melted butter

Soak mushrooms in water and wine until soft, about 1 hour. In a heavy kettle over medium heat, sauté onions in 6 tablespoons of the butter until limp. Add rice and cook and stir for 3 to 4 minutes. Add 1 cup of the hot broth and allow to gently boil, stirring often, until broth is absorbed. Add remaining broth, 1 cup at a time, and repeat. Add mushrooms with liquid and cook until rice is tender and almost dry (add a little more broth if necessary). Stir in the remaining 3 tablespoons butter and ½ cup Parmesan. Serve on hot plates or in soup plates. Pass melted butter and additional Parmesan to add according to taste. Makes 3 or 4 main-course or 6 accompaniment servings.

SUGGESTED ACCOMPANIMENTS:
Ripe tomatoes
Green salad with oil-vinegar dressing
Grissini
Dry white table wine

BARLEY-AND-MUSHROOM PILAF
TURKEY

If the budget allows, sauté a few more chicken livers in butter and serve on the side as a garnish.

> 1 *cup pearl barley*
> 4 *tablespoons butter*
> 3 *cups chicken broth*
> 1½ *cups finely chopped onions*
> ¼ *pound chicken livers, rinsed, dried, and finely chopped*
> ¼ *pound mushrooms, thinly sliced*
> *Salt and freshly ground black pepper*
> ¼ *cup plain yogurt*
> 2 *tablespoons finely chopped fresh parsley*
> 2 *ounces natural Gruyère or Emmenthal cheese,*
> *shredded (½ cup)*

In a heavy saucepan or kettle over low heat, sauté barley in 1 tablespoon of the butter, stirring frequently, until barley turns golden brown. Heat broth to boiling and pour over. Cover and simmer slowly without stirring until barley is tender, about 1½ hours. Meantime, in a heavy frying pan over medium heat, sauté onions in remaining 3 tablespoons butter until tender and golden. Add livers and sauté until they turn brown. Add mushrooms and sauté about 5 minutes more. Stir in ¾ teaspoon salt and ⅛ teaspoon pepper. When barley is tender, stir in half of the mushroom mixture, the yogurt, and parsley. Correct seasoning. Turn into a buttered 1½-quart casserole. Spread remaining mushroom mixture over top, and sprinkle with cheese. Bake in a 350° oven until cheese melts and is slightly crusted over, about 20 to 25 minutes. Makes 4 main-dish or 6 accompaniment servings.

SUGGESTED ACCOMPANIMENTS:
Green salad
Light dry red wine

DANISH BLUE CHEESE AND RICE HOT SALAD

DENMARK

It is important to add the blue-cheese cubes cold and last, so that they will barely melt, remaining instead as distinctive nuggets through the baking.

When serving the salad, you might offer black pepper. Any leftovers are good as a cold rice salad.

⅔ *cup long-grain white rice, cooked just until tender, rinsed, and drained*
2 *tablespoons melted butter*
2 *tablespoons fresh lemon juice*
1 *teaspoon dry mustard*
3 *tablespoons minced green onions with part of green tops*
1 *cup commercial sour cream*

3 *hard-cooked eggs, coarsely grated*
2 *small cans (2¼ ounces each) sliced black olives, drained*
3 *ounces firm cold blue cheese (preferably Danish),*
 cut into ½-inch cubes
 Garnishes (see below)

Toss rice with butter, lemon juice, and mustard. Add onions, sour cream, eggs, and olives, and gently mix. Gently toss in blue cheese. Turn into a buttered baking dish, about 1½ quarts. Cover and bake in a 350° oven just until heated through, about 30 minutes. Possible top garnishes at serving time: tiny cooked shrimp, hard-cooked egg wedges, whole olives, fine slices of green onion tops. Makes 4 servings.

SUGGESTED ACCOMPANIMENTS:
Ripe tomato wedges
Large crisp sesame wafers
Beer

SWEDISH RICE

SWEDEN

The lady who gave me this recipe says that in her childhood home (Midwestern Swedish), this was often a supper main dish, in the same way that pancakes can make a supper. Recently, she served it as the main part of a family picnic. The dish is smooth and subtle.

½ *cup long-grain white rice, cooked until tender, rinsed,*
 and drained
2 *cups milk*
 Generous ⅛ teaspoon salt
3 *eggs, separated*
¾ *cup sugar*

½ *teaspoon cornstarch*
½ *teaspoon almond extract*
⅛ *teaspoon cream of tartar*
   Heavy (whipping) cream (optional)

Combine rice, milk, and salt in a heavy saucepan. Heat to boiling and gently boil, stirring, for 5 minutes. Remove from heat. Beat egg yolks. Beating constantly, add about ½ cup of the hot milk to yolks. Stirring, add yolk mixture to milk and rice. Mix 6 table-spoons of the sugar with the cornstarch; stir into rice mixture. Cook over medium heat, stirring constantly, until mixture thickens slightly and coats a silver spoon (do not let it boil). Remove from heat and stir in almond extract. Turn into a baking dish, about 1½ quarts. Beat egg whites with cream of tartar until foamy. Beat in remaining 6 tablespoons sugar, adding a table-spoon at a time, and beating until whites are stiff and glossy. Gently spread over rice, sealing well at edges. Bake in a 400° oven until golden brown, about 12 minutes. Let cool to warm or room temperature. Pass cream. Makes 4 supper or 6 dessert servings.

All Manner of Pastas

It seems almost a contradiction that fine pastas can be inexpensive. A caringly cooked pasta dish is such a queenly thing that it seems it would have to be royal in its price. But fine pastas are not expensive, yet give the effect of extravagance. This is partly because they are so outrageously delicious and partly because they are so elegant and artfully designed.

I admire the whole idea of pastas. They can provoke a cozy fantasy for me, with sauces cavorting over tender arcs of pasta, flat ribbons cuddling into cream, thread strands slipping into heady broths. Neither a pasta nor its sauce can do without the other. And a sublime pasta at its ultimate is almost too delightful to be real.

I appreciate the specificity of pastas—how each was contrived for a suitable kind of broth or saucing, how the right pasta and sauce can require each other so much and nudge together so splendidly, how the successful combinations show an intelligence behind them. A Roman chef chooses a flat fettuccine for the velvety al burro treatment with cream and butter and cheese. A Bolognese wants a wide lasagne to take a heavy sauce and cheese layering. A Neapolitan insists upon thin spaghetti strands for his sauce of sea clams. A Tuscan requires flat bite-size squares to show off a winy dark hare sauce.

It is not just the Italians who have plotted these stunning marriages of pasta and sauce. The Greek orzo, *which is football-shaped, is right for the loose tomato sauce in a lamb Giouvetsi. The Cantonese thin mein noodles do well for a quick stir-fry. The Japanese* udon *fills out a* dashi *broth. The German broad noodles lead to hearty chicken and noodles.*

I like to make my own dough for Italian pastas or German noodle dishes. But purchased fresh, Italian pastas or dried noodles are perfectly all right to use. You can usually interchange about equal weights of fresh and dry pastas.

*Whatever pasta you use, cook attentively in plenty of boiling salted water (I like to add a little oil for sheen and softness), and only until tender but still with some resistance and bite (*al dente *to the Italians). Then drain well and quickly sauce or cloak to prevent sticking.*

In this chapter, I am talking about pastas as a main course, not as a first course. These are not lead-ins to a further meal, as in a properly coursed Italian menu. So these can stand to be rather rich and the portions generous.

GREEN BEANS AND GREEN PASTA WITH WALNUT SAUCE

ITALY

The nut sauce for this pasta is Genoese. The way it sauces both pasta and Italian beans is my idea of something very good.

You have to pay attention to the cooking time of both the beans and the pasta, so that they will be ready—properly cooked and hot—at the same time. But the stir-together sauce needs no attendance whatever; you just spoon it over

*the hot pasta and beans and let their heat soften it into a
heady gloss.*

1 *pound fresh Italian (Romano) beans, ends trimmed,
cooked, uncovered, in boiling salted water until tender,
and drained well*
½ *pound fresh green tagliarini, cooked* al dente *in boiling
salted water with a little olive oil, and drained well*
Walnut Sauce (recipe below)

Arrange beans and tagliarini, side by side, on warm serving plates
or platter. Spoon sauce over. Makes 4 main-course servings.

Walnut Sauce. Stir together 1⅓ cups coarsely ground walnuts, ½ cup coarsely ground pine nuts, 2 tablespoons fine soft
crumbs from Italian (or other) bread, ¾ cup olive oil, 2 large
pressed cloves garlic, ¼ cup heavy (whipping) cream, ¼ teaspoon
crumbled dried marjoram, and ½ teaspoon salt.

SUGGESTED ACCOMPANIMENTS:
Green salad with thin prosciutto or mild coppa slices alongside
Italian bread
Fresh dry white wine, as a Riesling, or almost any young dry
white without wood overtones

WINE MUSHROOM TAGLIATELLE

ITALY

*This way of cooking mushrooms, which renders them un-
usually nutty and meaty tasting, takes a little time—maybe
twenty minutes.*

1½ *pounds very thinly sliced fresh mushrooms*
½ *cup butter*
⅔ *cup dry white table wine*

1 *pressed clove garlic*
½ *cup finely chopped fresh parsley*
6 *ounces hot fresh wide tagliatelle* or *fettuccine, cooked*
    al dente *in boiling salted water with a little olive oil,*
    and drained well
    Black pepper in a grinder

In a large, heavy frying pan over medium-high heat, sauté mush-rooms in butter until they are deep golden and almost toasted, the butter browns slightly, and all mushroom liquid disappears. Add wine and garlic and continue cooking, stirring occasionally, until wine reduces almost completely. Remove from heat and stir in parsley. Add tagliatelle and gently toss to mix. Pass black pep-per. Makes 2 main-course or 4 first-course servings.

SUGGESTED ACCOMPANIMENTS:
Green salad
Sliced ripe tomatoes or cold sliced oranges sprinkled with basil
Dry fully flavored Riesling or other dry fresh white wine

PESTO PASTA AND PEAS

ITALY

Joseph Henry Jackson used to like this enough to title it affectionately "Knees and Poodles" (peas and noodles). His wife used to follow her family's Genoese tradition and serve it for special occasions because it is so pretty. Her grand-mother used to make it with green beans instead of peas.
*   This dish is for summertime when fresh peas and basil are in season.*

12 *ounces fresh tagliarini, cooked* al dente *in boiling salted water with a little olive oil, and drained well*
    Pesto (recipe below)

About ⅓ cup hot chicken broth
1 to 1½ cups shelled fresh or tiny frozen peas,
  cooked and drained
Freshly grated Parmesan cheese
About ¼ cup finely chopped fresh parsley

Toss hot tagliarini and pesto with enough broth to loosen the mixture, the peas, and ¼ cup Parmesan. Sprinkle with parsley. Pass additional Parmesan. Makes 4 main-course or 8 first-course servings.

Pesto. Put into blender container ¾ cup olive oil, 2 to 3 large peeled cloves garlic, ¼ cup freshly grated Parmesan, and 2 cups fresh basil leaves (pack loosely to measure). Whirl until smooth.

SUGGESTED ACCOMPANIMENTS:
Sliced ripe tomatoes
Italian bread
Dry white wine

CHUCK'S 104TH ZUCCHINI RECIPE

ITALY

"Chuck" is Chuck Williams, an owner of one of the finest cookware shops in the country.
  Add the Parmesan lightly. It should just nudge the sweetness of the zucchini, not overshadow it.

2 large cloves garlic, peeled and split
½ cup olive oil
¼ cup minced shallots
⅔ pound small unpeeled zucchini, finely diced
  (less than ¼ inch)

1 *to* 1½ *ounces Italian coppa or prosciutto or*
  Canadian bacon, finely diced
6 *ounces fresh tagliatelle or tagliarini, cooked* al dente *in*
  boiling salted water with a little olive oil, and
  drained well
  Salt and freshly ground black pepper
  Freshly grated Parmesan cheese

In a large, heavy frying pan over medium-high heat, sauté garlic in oil for 1 or 2 minutes. Add shallots and sauté until limp. Add zucchini and sauté until barely tender-crisp, about 3 to 4 minutes. Stir in coppa and heat through. Remove garlic. Add tagliatelle, toss, and add salt and pepper to taste. Sprinkle lightly with Parmesan. Makes 2 main-course or 4 first-course servings.

SUGGESTED ACCOMPANIMENTS:
Sliced ripe tomatoes
Full dry white wine

LUXURIOUS LASAGNE

ITALY

With this plan for making lasagne, you can have your meat and eat it too. The roast of beef cooks with the sauce ingredients to impart its rich beef flavor, but it does not go into the sauce; it is set aside to be used another time as cold sliced beef.

This recipe takes time. You can assemble the dish ahead— up to the point of topping with butter and cream—and refrigerate it or freeze it before baking. If chilled, allow additional baking time. If frozen, thaw before baking.

Tomato Sauce (recipe below)
Cooked Pasta (recipe below)

1 *cup ricotta cheese*
1½ *cups freshly grated Parmesan cheese*
2 *tablespoons butter*
2 *tablespoons heavy (whipping) cream*
Parsley sprigs

Spread one-fifth of the tomato sauce over bottom of a 13- by 9-inch baking pan. Place one-fourth of the pasta (cut to fit pan if necessary) side by side in pan over sauce. Spoon on one-fifth more of the sauce. Dot with one-third of the ricotta and sprinkle with one-fourth of the Parmesan. Repeat layering of sauce, pasta, and cheeses three more times except omit ricotta in top layer. Dot top with butter and drizzle with cream. Bake in a 350° oven until heated through and bubbling, about 45 minutes. Let stand for 10 minutes, then cut into squares to serve. Garnish each servings with a sprig of parsley. Makes 6 to 8 main-course servings.

Tomato Sauce. Rub a 3½-pound boneless beef rump roast with salt and freshly ground black pepper to season. In a large, heavy kettle, brown meat on all sides in 1 tablespoon olive oil. Add 2 cups finely chopped onions and sauté in drippings until limp. Stir in ¼ cup finely chopped celery, ¼ cup shredded peeled carrot, ¼ cup finely chopped fresh parsley, and 1½ cups dry red table wine. Simmer, stirring occasionally, until wine is completely reduced. Add 2 cans (1 pound, 12 ounces each) peeled whole tomatoes, drained and broken up (*or* 6 large ripe tomatoes, peeled and coarsely chopped), 2 cans (8 ounces each) tomato sauce, ¼ teaspoon ground sage, ⅛ teaspoon crumbled dried thyme, and ⅛ teaspoon sugar. Simmer very slowly, uncovered, stirring occasionally, until sauce is thick and even in consistency, about 3 to 4 hours. Remove meat and set aside for another use. Scald ¾ cup heavy (whipping) cream, and stir in.

Cooked Pasta. Cut about 10 ounces homemade or fresh pasta into 8 sheets, each about 12 by 4 inches. Cook strips *al dente,* two at a time, in a shallow wide pan of boiling salted water with a little olive oil. Lift out and lay flat on clean cloths to drain.

(Or cook 8 to 10 ounces packaged dried lasagne noodles *al dente* in boiling salted water with a little olive oil; drain.)

SUGGESTED ACCOMPANIMENTS:
Fresh lettuce and tender spinach salad
Bright dry red table wine

ROSEMARY PASTA

ITALY

To do this ideally, have fresh rosemary and a source of excellent fresh Italian pork sausage. Then you can arrange the pasta with big diagonal cuts of the sausage alongside. I plan on about 4 ounces mild Italian fresh pork sausage for two servings. To prepare, simply bake in a buttered shallow pan in a 350° oven for 30 minutes, turning once. You can use dried rosemary, and you can side the pasta with an Italian meat sauce instead of sausage. Go very easy on the rosemary. It can quickly overcome the pasta.

½ *cup butter*
1 *large pressed clove garlic*
¼ *teaspoon fresh or dried rosemary needles*
8 *ounces fresh tagliarini or tagliatelle, cooked* al dente
   in boiling salted water with a little olive oil, and
   drained well
   Freshly ground black pepper
   Salt

Melt 2 tablespoons of the butter in a small pan. Add garlic and rosemary and heat until butter bubbles. Cut remaining butter into small pieces and partially melt in a large warm bowl. Add tagliarini and garlic butter and toss to mix. Add a generous grinding of black pepper, and salt if you wish. Makes 2 main-course or 4 first-course servings.

SUGGESTED ACCOMPANIMENTS:
Roasted mildly spiced Italian fresh pork sausages
Green salad
Light bright red wine
Chilled sliced oranges

HAM PATCHES
(Schinkenfleckerln) AUSTRIA

This dish comes from Austria's Tyrol. It is a simple tossed sauté intended for supper—with beer, cold applesauce, and a leaf-lettuce salad dressed with oil and vinegar and salt and pepper. For some, the treasures of this dish are the crispy parts that stick to the bottom of the pan.

1½ *to* 2 *cups finely chopped onions*
½ *cup butter*
¼ *pound thinly sliced well-smoked ham, cut into*
   1*-inch squares*
6 *ounces wide egg noodles, cooked* al dente *in boiling salted water, rinsed, and drained well*
   Salt and freshly ground black pepper

In a large, heavy frying pan over medium-high heat, sauté onions in about 3 tablespoons of the butter until tender and browned; remove from pan. Add remaining butter to pan and heat until it foams and begins to brown. Add ham, then noodles, and sauté over high heat until lightly browned (turn frequently but allow some parts to brown well and slightly crisp on edges). Stir in onions, heat through, and season very generously with salt and pepper. Makes 4 servings.

BAKED MACARONI AND MEAT SQUARES
(Pastitsio)   GREECE

This recipe came straight from Greece but thirdhand: I got the recipe from Loni Kuhn; Loni got the recipe from her friend Elaine; Elaine got the recipe by watching her Greek aunt cook the dish. The aunt was one of those who would just as soon not tell the secrets of her kitchen activities, so Elaine's watching was furtive and her culinary curiosity was expediently controlled.

I have suggested that you use either feta or Parmesan cheese. Feta is the more authentic cheese, but I prefer the Parmesan.

A thin puff of the custard sauce makes a soft top layer.

1 *egg*
½ *teaspoon salt*
½ *pound elbow macaroni, cooked* al dente *in boiling salted water, drained, rinsed under cold running water, and drained well again*
    Meat Sauce (recipe below)
½ *pound feta cheese (preferably imported) or* ⅓ *cup freshly grated Parmesan cheese*
    Custard Sauce (recipe below)

Beat egg and salt together well; toss with macaroni. Spread half of the mixture over bottom of a well-buttered 13- by 9-inch baking pan. Cover with the meat sauce. Top with remaining macaroni. Sprinkle with half the cheese. Bake in a 350° oven for 15 minutes. Pour custard sauce evenly over and sprinkle with remaining cheese. Return to oven and bake for 40 minutes more. Let cool for about 20 minutes, then cut into squares. Makes 6 servings.

Meat Sauce. In a heavy kettle, brown 1 pound ground beef chuck until crumbly. Add 2 cups finely chopped onions and sauté until limp. Stir in 1 large can (15 ounces) tomato sauce, 1 can (6 ounces) tomato paste, ⅓ cup dry red wine, 2 pressed cloves garlic, ½ teaspoon crumbled dried oregano, ½ teaspoon crumbled dried basil, 1 teaspoon salt, ¼ teaspoon freshly ground black pepper, and a scant ⅛ teaspoon ground cinnamon. Cover and simmer, stirring occasionally, until blended and thickened, about 45 minutes.

Custard Sauce. In a heavy saucepan, melt 4 tablespoons butter and stir in 4 tablespoons flour to make a smooth paste. Gradually add 2 cups milk, cooking and stirring until sauce is smooth and thickened; simmer, stirring, for about 5 minutes more. Stir in ½ teaspoon salt, ⅛ teaspoon freshly ground pepper, and ⅛ teaspoon ground nutmeg. Remove from heat. Beat 2 eggs well. Gradually whisk hot sauce into eggs.

SUGGESTED ACCOMPANIMENTS:
Fresh leaf spinach and leaf lettuce salad
Bright dry red wine

ELABORATED NOODLE BOWL

JAPAN

In Japan, a whole meal may often be a bowl of noodles swimming in hot broth and topped with a colorful assortment of plain foods—often leftovers. There, the proportion of noodles to toppers might be greater than in this recipe. You can shift or substitute the toppings to your taste.

You can make this with all ingredients right from your supermarket. But to be most authentic, use dashi (fish-and-seaweed broth) for the liquid. You can buy it in instant packets in Oriental and specialty food shops; brew according to package directions. Use Japanese udon noodles. Sprinkle the finished bowl with a Japanese condiment called shichimi togarashi; *it is made up of hot chilies, toasted sesame seeds, Japanese pepper, and dried orange peel.*

Cook whatever noodles you use according to their type and package directions; time them to be done when the broth is ready.

5 *cups* dashi or *chicken broth*
1 *teaspoon soy sauce*
1 *teaspoon salt*
2 *frying chicken thighs*
2 *carrots, peeled and sliced* 1/4 *inch thick*
4 *large shrimp, shelled and deveined*
20 *fresh Chinese edible-pod (sugar) peas, ends and strings removed, or* 3/4 *cup fresh or frozen green peas*
1/2 *pound uncooked Japanese* udon *noodles or thin Chinese mein noodles or spaghetti, cooked and drained*
1 *hard-cooked egg, quartered*
2 *green onions with green tops, very thinly sliced*
Shichimi togarashi or *crushed dried hot red chilies (optional)*

Put *dashi,* soy sauce, salt, and chicken into a large saucepan. Heat to boiling, then cover and simmer until chicken is tender, about 20 minutes. Remove chicken, discard skin and bones, and cut meat into neat, thin lengthwise slices. Return chicken to broth along with carrots. Cover and simmer for 5 minutes more. Add shrimp and peas; simmer until shrimp turn pink and are opaque throughout, about 3 minutes. Divide hot noodles among 4 warm large bowls. With a slotted spoon, lift foods from broth and arrange some of each in separate little piles on top of noodles. Center each serving with an egg wedge. Sprinkle with onions. Ladle broth over. Sprinkle with *shichimi togarashi,* if desired. Makes 4 servings.

MALAYAN HOT TOSSED SALAD
(Bah Mee)   MALAYA

You stir-fry this so quickly and lightly that it is nearly salad-like, even though it contains noodles, ham, and chicken. There is no denying that it takes time to prepare all the ingredients, but the cooking time is ultrashort.

When they make this dish at restaurants, the cooks season it with a chili sauce from the Philippines. When you are out of easy reach of such an exotic addition, you can use Tabasco and a good dash of sugar, as below. You can buy oyster sauce in Chinese markets.

Cook this very fast to keep the vegetables crisp, sweet, and crunchy.

½ cup chicken broth
¼ cup oyster sauce
 3 large pressed cloves garlic
¼ teaspoon hot-pepper sauce
 1 teaspoon sugar
 3 tablespoons soy sauce
¼ cup peanut or other salad oil
 1 whole frying chicken breast, skinned and boned (6 to 8
    ounces meat), cut into strips 2 inches long and ¼
    inch wide
 3 to 4 ounces chicken livers, rinsed, dried, and cut into
    ½-inch pieces
 4 to 5 ounces well-smoked cooked hams, cut into
    julienne strips
 6 green onions with green tops, cut into julienne strips
 1 cup julienne strips of celery
¼ pound Chinese edible-pod (sugar) peas, ends and strings
    removed, cut into julienne strips
¼ pound bean sprouts

8 *peeled fresh* or *drained canned water chestnuts, sliced*
⅛ *inch thick*
⅓ *pound uncooked thin Chinese mein noodles* or *fine
spaghetti, cooked* al dente *in boiling salted water,
rinsed, and drained*
1 *egg*

Combine broth, oyster sauce, garlic, hot-pepper sauce, sugar, and
2 tablespoons soy sauce. Heat oil in a wok or very large, heavy
frying pan over high heat. Add chicken and livers and sauté until
they turn color. Stir in ham. Add onions, celery, peas, sprouts,
and water chestnuts, and toss to mix. Add noodles and broth
mixture. Cook and turn until heated through. Beat egg with
remaining soy sauce, pour over, and cook and turn to heat and to
glaze all ingredients. Makes 4 servings.

NOTE: Cut julienne strips of ham, green onions, celery, and
Chinese peas 2 inches long and ⅛ inch wide.

SUGGESTED ACCOMPANIMENT:
Fruity rosé wine or beer

A Little Shellfish
Can Go a Long Way

A delicacy is more precious when it is rare. This is a good thing to remember when the price of shellfish is high and you can have but a little. Then your joys in those tender little packets of seafood should be greater than ever.

Everything about the taste and texture of shellfish is delicate. So it is entirely appropriate to put shellfish into cooking in a delicate way. In the case of less costly cooking, this means with a light hand. The trick is to background the shellfish so that it shows the best. That usually means subtle settings that give attention to the shellfish—such enhancing and supporting things as soft eggs, buttered bread, ivory rice, velvety lettuce, succulent eggplant.

Doing without is better than using shellfish that has not been brought to you in the fervor of freshness. So if you cannot get fresh, fresh shellfish, use perfectly frozen shellfish.

ALMOND OYSTERS

FRANCE

The seasonings recall those typical for escargots—*parsley, garlic, butter.*
    If you use the larger Pacific oysters, give them the longer baking time.

  2 large pressed cloves garlic
  10 tablespoons melted butter
  2 jars (10 or 12 ounces each) Eastern or Pacific oysters, drained and patted dry
     About 3/16 teaspoon salt
     About ¼ teaspoon freshly ground black pepper
  4 tablespoons finely chopped fresh parsley
  3 cups fine soft bread crumbs (preferably sourdough French)
  ½ cup sliced almonds
  2 tablespoons butter

Mix garlic with the 10 tablespoons butter. Dip oysters in garlic butter and arrange in a single layer in a shallow baking dish. Sprinkle with salt, pepper, and parsley. Toss bread crumbs with remaining garlic butter and sprinkle over oysters. Bake in a 350° oven for 20 to 25 minutes (if necessary to lightly brown crumbs, slip under broiler for a few moments). Meantime, sauté almonds in the 2 tablespoons butter until lightly toasted; turn over baked oysters. Makes 4 generous servings.

SUGGESTED ACCOMPANIMENT:
Burgundy-type dry white wine

MUSTARD, SWEET ONION, AND SHRIMP

USA

*You eat these marinated arcs as an open-faced sandwich—
thickly piled onto bread to eat either out of hand or with
knife and fork. Or they can make a supper another way—
spooned into large peeled avocado half shells set on beds of
lettuce and accompanied with tomatoes and cold beer.*

  1 *large sweet onion*
  1 *pound tiny shelled cooked shrimp*
½ *cup olive oil*
¼ *cup white wine vinegar*
  2 *tablespoons Dijon-style mustard*
    Thin slices of dark bread, as farm- or Bavarian-style
    pumpernickel
    Black pepper in a grinder

Cut onion, top to bottom, into ⅛-inch-wide wedge slices and
break apart into a bowl. Add shrimp. Beat oil, vinegar, and
mustard together until smooth and slightly thickened. Pour over
onion and shrimp, and turn to coat well. Cover and chill for 12
to 24 hours; turn once or twice. Pass shrimp mixture for each
person to spoon onto bread. Pass pepper to be used generously.
Makes 4 to 6 servings.

SUGGESTED ACCOMPANIMENTS:
Light green salad
Cherry tomatoes
Dry or off-dry Gewürztraminer

PRAWN SOUP
(Chupe de Camarones)   PERU

This is a sweet and delicate soup. If you want to fill it out more, add an egg or two just before adding parsley: Break egg into broth at edge of kettle and slowly sweep it through the soup with a spoon so that the egg coagulates in large pieces.

Eat the corn with your fingers.

1 cup finely chopped onions
3 tablespoons olive oil
3 cups water
2 large pressed cloves garlic
¾ teaspoon crumbled dried oregano
⅛ teaspoon crushed dried hot red peppers
   Salt
¼ teaspoon freshly ground black pepper
2 medium-sized potatoes (about ¾ pound), peeled and
   quartered
¼ cup long-grain white rice
1 cup milk
2 teaspoons sugar
2 ears fresh corn, cut into 1-inch slices
1 pound fillets of red snapper or sea bass or rock cod or
   other rockfish or lean white fish, cut into 2-inch squares
½ cup shelled fresh or frozen peas
8 medium-sized shrimp, shelled and deveined
½ cup finely chopped fresh parsley

In a large kettle, sauté onions in oil until limp. Add water, garlic, oregano, red peppers, 1½ teaspoons salt, the black pepper, and potatoes. Heat to boiling. Stir in rice. Cover and simmer until potatoes and rice are just tender, about 20 minutes. Add milk and sugar and heat to simmering. Add corn, fish, and peas. Cover and simmer for 3 minutes. Add shrimp and simmer until shrimp are pink and fish flesh barely separates when tested with a dinner knife, about 3 minutes. Stir in parsley, add salt to taste, and serve immediately. Makes 4 servings.

SUGGESTED ACCOMPANIMENTS:
Light leaf lettuce salad
Tomatoes
Light beer

SHRIMP IN GARLIC CRUMBS
(Acorda) PORTUGAL

I have eaten and observed the making of this original dish many times in Portugal, and I often serve it to guests at home.

Last spring, after a six-year absence from Portugal, I returned to my still-favorite little Lisbon restaurant to find that açorda was still as popular as ever. There at Restaurante Porto de Abrigo, at both lunch and dinner, this was the dish that the local gourmets would order with beer. There the açorda was served with the eggs already added and the mélange was ladled out of a great casserole. Here at home, I like the ritual and show of the last-minute egg addition and the chance to see and hear the sizzling crumbs cook the eggs.

A Portuguese açorda is really a dry soup, softer and less toasty-crisp than my version. It might be made of other shellfish, pork, or chicken.

About 1 loaf whole-wheat bread
6 large crushed cloves garlic
1 cup olive oil
½ pound shelled and cooked tiny shrimp
½ cup finely chopped fresh coriander

½ *cup finely chopped fresh parsley*
   Salt and freshly ground black pepper
4 *eggs*
   Lemon wedges

Trim crusts from bread and whirl bread in a blender or food processor to make 4 cups of fine crumbs. In a large shallow casserole or frying pan, heat garlic in oil in a 350° oven until garlic is golden. Stir in crumbs to coat with oil. Bake, stirring occasionally, until crumbs are very crisp and golden, about 25 to 30 minutes. Sprinkle with shrimp, coriander, parsley, and a generous amount of salt and pepper to taste. Take to the table, break eggs over the top, and stir just to mix. Serve immediately. Liberally squeeze on lemon juice as you eat. Makes 4 servings.

SUGGESTED ACCOMPANIMENTS:
Ripe tomatoes
Green salad
Cold beer

EAST INDIAN EGGPLANT-PRAWN SAUTE
INDIA

This supper almost turns on the zesty refreshment of limes. You squeeze their juice over the prawn sauté (just as surely as you grind on black pepper), the accompanying rice, and a ripe melon wedge.

A food-savvy doctor friend pronounced this dish as "bowling-over elegant." It is regal.

This amount will stretch to six servings if you have rice along with it. Chop the fresh coriander just before you use it.

3 *cups finely chopped onions*
1 *tablespoon ground coriander*
¼ *teaspoon ground turmeric*
   About ¼ teaspoon crushed dried hot red peppers

½ *cup butter*
6 *tablespoons olive oil*
1 *pound unpeeled eggplant, cut into* ½*-inch cubes*
Salt
2 *tablespoons finely grated fresh ginger*
5 *to* 6 *large pressed cloves garlic*
1 *pound large raw prawns (about* 12 *to* 15 *per pound),*
   shelled, deveined, and patted dry
4 *medium-sized ripe tomatoes, peeled, cut into eighths,*
   and seeded
1 *cup chopped fresh coriander* (cilantro or *Chinese parsley*)
   Lime wedges
   Black pepper in a grinder

In a large, heavy frying pan over medium-high heat, sauté onions, ground coriander, turmeric, and hot red peppers in butter and oil until onions are limp. Add eggplant and 1½ teaspoons salt, and sauté until eggplant is almost tender, about 5 minutes. Add ginger, garlic, and prawns, and turn to mix. Add tomatoes. Sauté, gently turning occasionally, just until prawns are pink and opaque throughout, about 5 to 8 minutes. Correct seasoning with salt. Sprinkle with fresh coriander. Garnish generously with lime wedges, and squeeze on juice to taste. Pass black pepper. Makes 4 servings.

SUGGESTED ACCOMPANIMENTS:
Hot buttered rice with lime wedges
Fresh melon with lime wedges
A very fully flavored dry white wine, or a dry rosé

QUITO SHRIMP IN CITRUS
(Ceviche de Langostinos)   ECUADOR

This is a first course in Ecuador and can be offered the same way here. Accompany with thin, crisp buttered toast, and pass a bowl of ripe avocados which have been mashed nearly smooth with fresh lime juice and salt to season; spread avocado mix thickly on toast. Provide cold light beer. Serve scrambled eggs later, with more toast and avocado mix.

½ *cup prepared chili sauce*
1¼ *teaspoons grated fresh orange peel*
⅓ *cup fresh orange juice*
⅓ *cup fresh lemon juice*
⅓ *cup olive oil*
1 *teaspoon salt*
About ½ teaspoon freshly ground black pepper
½ *teaspoon sugar*
1 *or 2 drops hot-pepper sauce (more if you want a hotter sauce)*
1 *large pressed clove garlic*
4 *teaspoons finely grated sweet red onion*
½ *pound tiny cooked and shelled shrimp*
Toasted corn kernels (corn nuts)
Roasted shelled peanuts

Stir together all except last three ingredients. Fold in shrimp. Chill. Spoon shrimp into individual shallow dishes. Pass a small bowl of corn kernels and one of peanuts for each person to add to taste. Makes 6 first-course servings.

BAY OYSTER STEW

USA

4 *ounces sliced lean bacon, cut into small pieces*
1½ *cups finely chopped onions*
1 *medium-sized potato (½ pound), peeled, quartered, and thinly sliced*
2 *cups water*
Salt

A Little Shellfish Can Go a Long Way

1½ *pints Eastern* or *small Pacific oysters with liquor*
  2 *cups milk*
    Dash of hot-pepper sauce
    Freshly ground black pepper
 ½ *cup finely chopped fresh parsley*
  3 *tablespoons butter*

In a large, heavy kettle over medium heat, cook bacon until crisp; remove with a slotted spoon and drain. Add onions to kettle and sauté until golden. Add potato, water, and ¼ teaspoon salt, cover, and boil until potato is just tender. Return bacon to kettle, cover, and simmer for 5 minutes. Drain oysters. Add liquor and milk to kettle and heat just to boiling. Add oysters and simmer until oyster edges curl, about 3 minutes. Add hot-pepper sauce, salt and pepper to season. Stir in parsley. Ladle into warm bowls. Top each serving with a pat of butter. Makes 4 servings.

SUGGESTED ACCOMPANIMENTS:
Sliced ripe tomatoes
Green salad (optional)
Crisp toast
Dry white wine

Fine Fish

I feel only sincere sympathy for those who do not live near the sea or a lake or a river where they can get fresh local fish, and for those who neglect to buy and cook fish when available.

One reason that fish is a favorite of mine is that it is so easy to cook. Given the pure tastes and texture of fish, it is difficult to do wrong when cooking a fish except by over-cooking. If you know how not to overcook, you know how to cook fish, because a fresh fish brings all the other qualities to you. You could actually fry, poach, bake, steam, or grill a perfectly fresh fish without an iota of saucing or seasoning and come up with something delicious—if you did not do the fish in by too much cooking.

Just-doneness is a fleeting moment in fish cookery. You have to pay attention to catch that moment. No timing will work universally. You have to test each fish you are cooking. Two different fish of the same species and size may cook differently. And that is to say nothing of timing variations that happen because of different kinds of fish, ways of cooking, utensil sizes and weights, qualities of heat, modes of preparation, etc.

Most recipes say the fish is done when the flesh flakes easily when tested with a fork. By then a fish is too done for me, so my test for doneness is a little different. I touch the fish with the tip of a dinner knife. If the flesh barely separates and still clings slightly to the bone (if any), I consider it done.

But when to start testing? James Beard has cooked fish and fish and fish and researched and timed and tested. He has come up with a sound general guideline for how long to cook a whole fish or part of a fish. It works almost invariably. Cook a fish of whatever size by whatever method for ten minutes per inch of thickness at the thickest part of the fish. I recommend it as your overall principle to precede your precise testing.

Once you find the fish just done, get it right out of the hot cooking vessel and onto a warm serving platter or plate. Pray do not put it on a hot plate or the cooking will go on, and the fish will become as sad from overcooking on a sizzling platter as it might have on the stove or grill.

CUMIN-BUTTER SNAPPER

TUNISIA

2 pounds fillets of red snapper or *rock cod* or *other rockfish*
*   or *sea bass*
Salt
Freshly ground black pepper
About ½ teaspoon ground cumin
1 *tablespoon finely minced green onions (white part only)*
5 *tablespoons butter*
*   Sprigs of fresh coriander* or *flat-leaf parsley*
*   Lime wedges*

Season each side of fish fairly generously with salt and pepper. Rub surfaces with cumin. Arrange fish in a single layer in a well-buttered shallow baking dish. Sprinkle with onions. Dot with butter. Bake in a 350° oven until fish flesh barely separates when tested with a dinner knife, about 15 to 20 minutes (20 to 25 minutes for thicker fillets of bass). Baste occasionally with pan juices. Serve with all juices spooned over. Garnish with fresh coriander sprigs and lime wedges. Squeeze on drops of lime juice only if you wish. Makes 4 servings.

SUGGESTED ACCOMPANIMENTS:
Cooked fresh leaf spinach
Dry white table wine with good acid, as a dry Sauvignon Blanc
    or Pinot Blanc

BAKED BUTTERFISH WITH NEW POTATOES AND CAPER SAUCE

USA

On the Pacific coast, butterfish also go by the names of black cod and sablefish. Butterfish bear an unlikely pair of charac-

teristics: *they are one of the least expensive fish to buy, and they are about the most elegantly fleshed.*

> 2 *pounds butterfish fillets*
> *Salt*
> *Freshly ground black pepper*
> ⅓ *cup melted butter*
> 12 *hot small boiled unpeeled new potatoes*
> *Caper Sauce* (recipe below)

Wipe fish dry with a damp cloth. Season lightly with salt and generously with pepper. Arrange in a single layer in a shallow baking dish. Pour butter over. Bake in a 350° oven just until flesh barely separates when tested with a dinner knife, about 12 to 15 minutes; baste once or twice with pan juices. Lift to serving plates, and pour pan juices over. Arrange potatoes alongside. Spoon part of the caper sauce over both fish and potatoes. Pass remaining sauce. Makes 4 servings.

Caper Sauce. Melt ½ cup butter. Add 2 tablespoons drained capers, ⅓ cup finely chopped fresh parsley, and ½ teaspoon fresh lemon juice, and barely heat through.

SUGGESTED ACCOMPANIMENT:
Bright dry red wine, as a Grignolino

SWEET-VEGETABLE MARINATED FISH
(Escabeche) PORTUGAL

Every seafaring country has its marinated fish. And every lover of fish gets to choose his favorite. Mine is the escabeche *of Portugal. It is more subtle than most other marinated fish I am familiar with, and it has a luxurious fresh-vegetable sweetness. The accompaniments just have to be baked or ember-roasted potatoes and a bright red wine.*

> 2 *pounds fillets of sea bass* or *red snapper* or *other rockfish*
> or *other firm and large-textured white-fleshed fish*
> *Salt and freshly ground black pepper*
> *Olive oil*
> 2 *large sweet onions, very thinly sliced*
> 2 *large carrots, peeled and coarsely grated*
> 2 *large crushed cloves garlic*
> 1 *large bay leaf, crumbled*
> ¼ *teaspoon crushed dried hot red peppers*
> *About* ⅔ *cup mild white wine vinegar*

Wipe fish dry with a damp cloth and season generously with salt and pepper. In a heavy pan over medium to medium-high heat, fry fish in a generous amount of oil just until flesh barely separates when tested with a dinner knife. Remove fish from pan, let cool, remove any skin and bones, and break into large chunks. In a large frying pan, sauté onions in ¾ cup olive oil until tender. Stir in carrots, garlic, bay leaf, about 1½ teaspoons salt, ¼ teaspoon black pepper, the red peppers, and vinegar. Allow to cool. Arrange fish and onion mixture in alternate layers, beginning and ending with onion mixture, in a deep glass or earthenware bowl. Cover and chill for 2 to 4 days. Remove from refrigerator 1 to 2 hours before serving. Makes 6 servings.

SUGGESTED ACCOMPANIMENTS:
Potatoes baked or roasted in skins
Lettuce and watercress salad with oil-lemon juice dressing
(optional)
Bright dry red wine

GARLIC SNAPPER
(Huachinango en Ajo)   MEXICO

In Mexico as well as here, snapper is one of the most abundant and least expensive of fishes. Mexicans expertly fry the snapper in the garlic-pervaded oil, but I bake the snapper because I do not like to fry fish.

2 *pounds fillets of red snapper* or *rock cod* or *other rockfish*
Salt
Freshly ground black pepper
⅓ *cup olive oil*
6 *large cloves garlic, peeled and chopped into about*
⅛-*inch dice*
Fresh lime wedges

Wipe fish dry and season generously on both sides with salt and pepper. Heat oil in a small pan over medium-high heat until hot. Add garlic and cook, stirring, until crisp and golden. Strain garlic from oil and spread on paper towels. Arrange fish in a single layer in an oiled shallow baking dish. Pour garlic oil over. Bake in a 350° oven until fish flesh barely separates when tested with a dinner knife, about 15 to 20 minutes. Baste occasionally with pan juices. Serve with all juices spooned over. Sprinkle with reserved garlic. Garnish generously with lime wedges, and squeeze on juice to taste. Makes 4 servings.

SUGGESTED ACCOMPANIMENTS:
Lettuce and tomato salad
Warm tortillas
Beer

ORANGE RED SNAPPER, MEXICO CITY
MEXICO

Sauté the onions to deep gold in order to bring out their complete sweetness.

> 3 *cups finely chopped onions*
> 1 *cup olive oil*
> 1 *cup fine dices of peeled and seeded ripe tomatoes*
> ¼ *cup fresh orange juice*
>   *Salt*
> 4 *small whole red snappers (about 1 pound each), cleaned, scaled, heads removed if you wish; or 2 pounds fillets of red snapper*
> 12 *to 16 very thin slices of peeled fresh orange*
>   *Minced fresh parsley*
> 8 *small peeled hot boiled potatoes*

In a large, heavy frying pan over medium heat, sauté onions in oil until tender and deep golden, about 30 minutes. Remove from heat and stir in tomatoes, orange juice, and about 1½ teaspoons salt. Wipe fish dry. Season inside and out (or both surfaces) fairly generously with salt. Add fish to frying pan or arrange in a single layer in a large shallow baking pan, and spoon onion mixture over. Bake in a 350° oven until fish flesh barely separates when tested with a dinner knife, about 35 minutes for whole fish, 20 minutes for fillets. Baste occasionally. Serve fish with all juices spooned over. Garnish each serving with overlapping orange slices and a light sprinkling of parsley. Side with potatoes. Makes 4 servings.

SUGGESTED ACCOMPANIMENT:
Beer or very dry white table wine

FILLETS IN DILL SAUCE

GREECE

Be sure to use fresh or freshly dried herbs and follow the measurements as they are written.

4 pieces fillet of red snapper or striped bass or sea bass
  or lingcod or other nice large-fleshed sea fish,
  each ½ pound
¾ teaspoon salt
⅜ teaspoon freshly ground black pepper
½ cup olive oil
1½ tablespoons finely chopped fresh parsley
1 tablespoon very finely minced shallots
  About 2 tablespoons snipped fresh dill weed or
  ½ teaspoon crumbled dried dill weed
1/16 teaspoon crumbled dried oregano
¼ cup fresh lemon juice

Wipe fish dry with a damp cloth. Sprinkle both sides with salt and pepper. Arrange in a single layer in an oiled shallow baking dish. Sprinkle with oil, parsley, shallots, dill, and oregano. Bake in a 350° oven until fish flesh barely separates when tested with a dinner knife, about 15 to 25 minutes, depending upon thickness. Baste occasionally with pan juices. Lift fish to serving plate. Stir lemon juice into pan drippings. Pour all juices over fish. Makes 4 servings.

SUGGESTED ACCOMPANIMENTS:
Boiled new potatoes
Buttered green beans

Ripe tomatoes

A full-flavored dry white wine without wood overtones, such as a California Chardonnay or Pinot Blanc

DANISH FISH-PUDDING SOUFFLE

DENMARK

My thanks to gastronome John Ross and his fam , of Cambridge, Massachusetts, for this recipe.

> 6 *tablespoons butter*
> 10 *tablespoons all-purpose flour*
> 2 *cups milk*
>   *Flaked Dried Cod* (recipe below)
> 6 *eggs, separated*
> 1 *teaspoon freshly grated or ground nutmeg*
> ⅛ *teaspoon sugar*
>   *Salt and freshly ground white pepper to taste*
>   *Fine soft bread crumbs*
>   *Butter Sauce* (recipe below)

Melt butter in a heavy saucepan. Add flour and cook and stir to make a smooth paste. Gradually add milk, and whisk and stir until mixture is thickened and smooth. Simmer, whisking, for 5 minutes more. Stir in cod. Beat egg yolks, and gradually whisk into sauce along with nutmeg and sugar. Add salt if necessary and about ⅛ teaspoon pepper. Beat egg whites until stiff but not dry. Thoroughly fold one-third of the whites into fish sauce; lightly fold in remaining whites. Turn into a 2-quart soufflé dish that has been buttered and coated with crumbs. Bake in a 375° oven until puffed, set, and golden, about 35 minutes. Spoon out to serve immediately with butter sauce. Makes 6 servings.

Flaked Dried Cod. Soak ½ pound skinned and boned dried cod (or slightly more unboned cod) in cold water for 24 hours, until it is very moist throughout; change water two or three times. (Or freshen cod according to package directions.) Simmer cod, covered, in water to cover until tender, about 15 minutes; drain; remove skin and bones if necessary; flake finely.

Butter Sauce. Beat 1½ cups soft unsalted butter until fluffy. Gradually beat in 1½ tablespoons fresh lemon juice. Turn into serving bowl and sprinkle with freshly grated or ground nutmeg.

SUGGESTED ACCOMPANIMENTS:
Lightly cooked fresh spinach
Light beer

STEAMED ROCK COD, CANTONESE

CHINA

In a Cantonese restaurant, the chef often steams a rock cod for the finale of a many-coursed meal. It is wondrous to see the fish presented in its whole glory on a big, deep platter, settled into its natural and gingery juices and feathered with a froth of Chinese parsley.

At home, I find it easier to steam a fillet of cod, serve it as the feature of dinner, and present it the same as a whole fish. This is, in fact, about the simplest fish preparation I know. And I find it one of the best for celebrating the purity of tastes and appearance of a lovely thing from the sea. It is such a pleasure to have a fish without the usual clutter of Continental preparations.

Arrange your steaming setup in whatever way is easiest for you and your equipment. You'll need a large container with a tight-fitting lid, a rack, and a deep platter. Simplest for me is to put about an inch of water in the bottom of a wide, deep frying pan, put in three canning-lid rings as a steaming rack, set a nine-inch ovenware glass pie pan (with the fish in it) on the rings, and cover tightly to steam. The pie pan is deep enough to hold all the tasty juices that form during steaming, and it is simple to serve from. Do not over-steam the fish or its tender texture will toughen.

1-pound fillet of rock cod
½ teaspoon grated fresh ginger
½ teaspoon salt
About ¼ teaspoon freshly ground black pepper
2 tablespoons minced green onions with part of green tops
Chinese parsley (fresh coriander) sprigs

Rub fish on both sides with ginger and sprinkle with salt and pepper. Place in steaming plate or platter. Sprinkle with onions. Place on rack above gently boiling water. Cover tightly and steam until layers of fish flesh barely separate when tested with a dinner knife, about 15 minutes. Lift fish onto serving platter or plates, pour all juices over, and garnish generously with Chinese parsley. Serve fish with all juices. Makes 2 servings.

MASKED ARAB FISH

LEBANON

This dish is festive and colorful, and fresh enough to show off the good fish and a medley of textures. I would keep it for when company comes. It can be served at room temperature as well as hot.

You can purchase tahina (a paste of ground hulled sesame seeds) in Middle Eastern specialty shops.

2 cups finely chopped onions
Olive oil

2¼ *cups finely chopped green bell peppers*
1½ *cups ground walnuts*
   Salt and freshly ground black pepper
   Finely chopped fresh parsley
⅓ *cup fresh pomegranate seeds*
   2-*pound fillet of sea bass* or *striped bass, lingcod, rock*
   cod, or *other rockfish*
   Lemon Sesame Sauce (recipe below)
   Thin lemon slices

In a large frying pan over medium heat, sauté onions in ¾ cup oil until soft and golden. Stir in peppers and walnuts and sauté until peppers are barely tender, about 4 minutes. Remove from heat and stir in ¾ teaspoon salt, about ¾ teaspoon pepper, ¾ cup parsley, and half of the pomegranate seeds. Correct seasoning. Wipe fish dry with a damp cloth. Season both sides lightly with salt and pepper. Place in an oiled shallow baking dish. Spoon about 3 tablespoons olive oil evenly over top. Spoon walnut mixture over fish to cover. Bake in a 350° oven until fish flesh barely separates when tested with a dinner knife, about 20 to 30 minutes, depending upon fish thickness. Baste occasionally with pan juices. Spoon part of the sesame sauce over top, and sprinkle with 2 tablespoons parsley and the remaining pomegranate seeds. Garnish with lemon. Pass remaining sesame sauce. Makes 6 servings.

Lemon Sesame Sauce. In a deep bowl, stir together 1 cup *tahina* and 3 pressed cloves garlic. With a spoon, gradually beat in ½ cup fresh lemon juice, ½ cup cold water, and 1 teaspoon salt. If necessary to make sauce the consistency of thick mayonnaise: continue beating in cold water, adding it 1 tablespoon at a time; do not add more than ½ cup water. Correct seasoning.

SUGGESTED ACCOMPANIMENTS:
Fresh leaf spinach
Wilted cucumbers seasoned with a little dill and dressed lightly
   with olive oil

Arab bread

A dry California Sauvignon Blanc or other fresh but somewhat
firm dry white wine

Dried apricots poached with fresh vanilla bean or ginger or both

Crisp cardamom cookies

Thrifty Chickens

Chicken has managed a most clever accomplishment. It moved from being scarce and costly to abundant and cheap without losing stature or popularity. Its history in this country brought it through a change from being a rare bird, never to be eaten except on special occasions and Sundays, to a vastly available bird at easy prices and a possibility for most tables on any day.

This is not the way the world often works. So it would not be pessimistic to expect that familiarity would breed contempt. But with chicken, it seems rather that familiarity has bred more chicken, more ways to cook chicken, and more pleasure in eating chicken.

Chicken has achieved and retained its popularity by presenting all sorts of nice traits, not the least of which is the ability to come off as two quite different presentations: the extra-fine and elegant white meat of breasts and the dark meat of the rest of the bird. So cooks can offer chicken on two different levels, and almost as two different birds. (Many of us still hold out for dark-meat thighs and legs as the best part of the bird.)

Other pleasant traits for chicken are its readiness to be cooked by any method—poaching, broiling, barbecuing, grilling, roasting, frying; its agreeability to all kinds of dif-

ferent spicings, seasonings, and saucings; its succulent flesh, which is tasty enough to be interesting while mellow enough to appeal to many palates; its simplicity to handle and cook well; and its easy availability.

PARSLEY CREAM CHICKEN

NORWAY

2½-pound frying chicken, cut into serving pieces
About 3 tablespoons butter
¼ cup finely chopped fresh parsley
Salt and freshly ground white or black pepper
1 cup heavy (whipping) cream
Parsley sprigs

Rinse and dry chicken. Heat butter in a large, heavy frying pan over medium heat until it bubbles. Add chicken, dark pieces first, and sauté until golden on all sides, about 20 minutes. Stir chopped parsley into drippings, and season chicken very generously with salt and pepper. Pour cream over. Bake, uncovered, in a 275° oven until chicken is tender, about 1 hour; turn chicken once or twice. Remove chicken to a warm serving platter. Cook and stir juices in pan over high heat just to blend to a very thin sauce; pour over chicken. Garnish with parsley sprigs. Makes 4 servings.

SUGGESTED ACCOMPANIMENTS:
Boiled small new potatoes, parsley-buttered
Spring lettuce salad
Fresh tomatoes
Fruity white table wine

NEW ORLEANS JAMBALAYA

USA

Depending upon your kettle and rice and other variables,
you may need to add a little more broth during final baking
of the rice. But if you do so, add only as much as the rice
will absorb to cook tender.

3 *pounds frying chicken breasts and thighs*
(6 or more pieces)
4 *tablespoons* each *olive oil and butter*
1 *cup finely chopped onions*
1 *cup thinly sliced green onions with part of green tops*
1 *cup chopped celery*
1 *cup chopped green bell peppers*
3 *or 4 large pressed cloves garlic*
1 *tablespoon sugar*
2 *teaspoons salt*
½ *teaspoon freshly ground black pepper*
1¾ *teaspoons crumbled dried thyme*
1¼ *teaspoons crumbled dried basil*
   Generous pinch of cayenne (to taste)
3 *whole bay leaves*
1 *can (1 pound) peeled whole tomatoes, broken up*
1 *cup chicken broth*
½ *pound well-smoked cooked ham, cut into ½-inch cubes*
1½ *cups long-grain white rice*

Rinse and dry chicken. In a large, heavy kettle over medium-high heat, brown chicken in 2 tablespoons each of the oil and butter; do not crowd; remove when browned. Add remaining oil and butter to kettle. Add onions, green onions, celery, and green peppers, and sauté until limp. Stir in remaining ingredients except rice. Return chicken to kettle. Cover and simmer until chicken is just tender, about 30 minutes. Stir in rice. Bake, covered, in a 325° oven for 20 minutes. Gently stir. Bake, uncovered, until rice is tender, about 15 minutes more. Toss rice with a fork to fluff. Makes 6 servings.

SUGGESTED ACCOMPANIMENTS:
Green lettuce salad
French bread
Beer

LAUREL CHICKEN FROM GENOA

ITALY

2½-pound frying chicken, cut into serving pieces
  2 carrots, peeled and sliced diagonally into 1½-inch pieces
    Four 3-inch sprigs fresh rosemary or about ½ teaspoon
    crumbled dried rosemary
  2 whole bay leaves
    About 2 tablespoons olive oil
    About 2 tablespoons butter
    Salt and freshly ground black pepper
    About ¾ cup dry white table wine
  2 large pressed cloves garlic

Rinse and dry chicken. In a large, heavy frying pan over medium heat, sauté chicken, carrots, rosemary, and bay leaves in oil and butter until chicken is golden on all sides, about 20 to 25 minutes. Do not crowd chicken in pan when browning. If necessary, brown only part of the chicken at a time. Add breast pieces to brown after dark-meat pieces are about halfway brown. Season chicken generously with salt and pepper. Sprinkle with ¼ cup of the wine and add garlic. Continue cooking, turning chicken in pan juices, until chicken is tender, about 15 minutes. During cooking, sprinkle chicken with additional wine, 2 tablespoons at a time, whenever nearly all juices disappear. Remove chicken and carrots to warm serving platter. Add 4 tablespoons wine to pan, and cook and stir over high heat to loosen drippings and to blend and slightly reduce juices. Pour over chicken. Makes 4 servings.

SUGGESTED ACCOMPANIMENTS:
Salad of lettuce and sliced oranges with oil-vinegar dressing
White wine

PORTUGUESE BOILED DINNER DA SILVA
(Cozido à Portuguêsa) AZORES

Cozido à Portuguêsa *is the Portuguese boiled dinner, and it comes in as many forms as there are Portuguese cooks. Often it contains beef, ham, dried beans, two kinds of potatoes, cabbage, and carrots. But this version concentrates on the chicken and sausages. Though the rice is served separately, it is considered part of the dish. If you wish, you can add along with the spinach one medium-sized head of green cabbage, cut into twelve wedges and cored.*

You can use any remaining cooking broth as a first course for another meal or as soup stock base.

> ½ *pound* linguiça *or Polish sausages or other smoked pork garlic sausages, casings removed if necessary*
> 3½-*pound chicken, cut into serving pieces*
> 1 *large onion, peeled and quartered*
> 2 *celery stalks with leaves*
> 3 *tablespoons ground cumin*
> 1½ *teaspoons salt*
> ¼ *teaspoon freshly ground black pepper*
> 1 *cup long-grain white rice or short-grain pearl rice*
> 1 *can (1 pound) garbanzo beans, drained*
> 1½ *pounds fresh spinach (heavy stems removed before weighing), washed*
> *Finely chopped fresh coriander or parsley (optional)*
> *Coarse salt*
> *Black pepper in a grinder*

Pierce sausages in six places with a fork, cover with cold water, heat to boiling, simmer for 5 minutes, and drain. Put into a large, heavy kettle the sausages, chicken, onion, celery, cumin, salt, pepper, and about 5 cups cold water (to barely cover). Heat to boiling, then cover and simmer until chicken is tender, about 50 minutes. Remove about 2 cups of the broth, and in it, cook rice separately. Add garbanzos and spinach to large kettle and cook until spinach is tender, about 15 minutes. With a slotted spoon, remove chicken and vegetables and arrange on a warm serving platter. Cut sausages into ½-inch diagonal slices and arrange on platter. Spoon hot broth generously over to moisten. Sprinkle lightly with coriander. Serve rice alongside. Pass coarse salt and pepper in a grinder. Makes 6 servings.

SUGGESTED ACCOMPANIMENTS:
Sliced fresh oranges or pineapple
Beer or light bright dry red table wine

ALMOND CHICKEN WITH CHERRIES
NETHERLANDS

I use a special marinating preparation for the chicken in this recipe and in the one that follows because it transforms chicken flesh into something especially tender and flavorful. Do not let the steps of the marination put you off; you can do them almost without thought as you attend to other things. And you do not have to do the marinating just before cooking the chicken; you can complete the marinating steps, then cover and chill the chicken to hold it for an hour or so until you are ready to cook.

    Marinated Chicken Breast Fillets (recipe below)
    About 6 tablespoons butter
    3 *tablespoons brandy*
    1 *cup heavy (whipping) cream*
    About ¼ teaspoon ground nutmeg
    Salt and freshly ground black pepper
    3 *cups pitted fresh sweet dark cherries*
    ¾ *cup lightly toasted whole blanched almonds*

In a large, heavy frying pan over medium heat, sauté fillets in about 3 tablespoons of the butter just until they are opaque throughout and golden on both sides, about 8 minutes total (do not crowd in pan). With slotted spoon, remove to serving plates or platter, and keep warm. Add brandy to frying pan, and ignite. Spoon flames into the air until they die. Add cream and nutmeg to pan, increase heat to high and cook, stirring, until liquid reduces to the consistency of heavy cream. Correct seasoning with salt, pepper, and nutmeg. Pour sauce over chicken. Melt remaining butter over high heat in frying pan, add cherries, and swirl just until heated through; pour alongside chicken. Sprinkle with almonds. Makes 4 servings.

Marinated Chicken Breast Fillets. Split, skin, and bone 2 whole medium-sized frying chicken breasts (about 1 pound meat). Place each breast piece between two sheets of waxed paper, and pound with a meat pounder or the flat side of a cleaver or a rolling pin until breast is evenly ½ inch thick. Sprinkle chicken with ¾ teaspoon salt, ½ teaspoon freshly ground black pepper, and ¼ teaspoon ground nutmeg, and let stand for 20 minutes. Sprinkle with 4 teaspoons cornstarch and 4 teaspoons olive oil, turn to mix, and let stand for 20 minutes. Fold in 1 unbeaten egg white, and let stand for 30 minutes.

OLIVE CHICKEN

TUNISIA

Marinated Chicken Strips (recipe below)
4 tablespoons butter
2 to 3 tablespoons olive oil
1½ cups finely chopped onions
1¼ teaspoons ground cumin
½ teaspoon paprika

> ⅛ *teaspoon crushed dried hot red peppers (if you enjoy*
> *spicy hotness, increase this amount to taste)*
> 2 *large pressed cloves garlic*
> 2 *tablespoons fresh lemon juice*
> 6 *tablespoons chopped pitted green olives*
> 6 *tablespoons finely chopped fresh parsley*
> 16 *whole pitted green olives*
> 12 *small hot cooked peeled new potatoes*
> *Slender lemon wedges*

In a large, heavy frying pan over medium-high heat, sauté chicken strips in butter just until they are opaque throughout and a little golden, about 5 minutes. Remove chicken with a slotted spoon and set aside. Add olive oil to drippings in pan. Add onions and sauté until tender. Stir in cumin, paprika, hot peppers, garlic, lemon juice, chopped olives, and 4 tablespoons of the parsley. Heat through. Return chicken to pan, along with whole olives, and gently turn just to mix and heat through. Serve with potatoes alongside. Sprinkle chicken and potatoes with remaining parsley. Garnish with lemon wedges, and squeeze on juice to taste. Makes 4 servings.

Marinated Chicken Strips. Split, skin, and bone 2 whole medium-sized frying chicken breasts (about 1 pound meat). Slice chicken into strips no larger than 2½ by ⅜ inch. Sprinkle chicken with ¾ teaspoon salt, ½ teaspoon freshly ground black pepper, and ¼ teaspoon ground cumin, and let stand for 20 minutes. Sprinkle with 4 teaspoons cornstarch and 4 teaspoons olive oil, gently turn, and let stand for 20 minutes. Fold in 1 unbeaten egg white, and let stand for 30 minutes.

SUGGESTED ACCOMPANIMENTS:
Green salad with oil and vinegar dressing touched with
  Dijon-style mustard
Dry white table wine with full flavor and good acid, as a dry
  California Sauvignon Blanc

AUNT CLAIRE'S CHICKEN
AND CREAM NOODLES

USA

This old-fashioned meal is homespun and good. And you can make another meal from the same bird of chicken-rice soup: Do not pick the bones clean of meat, boil them with fresh water and seasonings to make a rich broth, remove bones and return all meat to broth, add rice and cook it until tender.

For the recipe below, you do not have to do the first five-minute chicken boiling, but it makes for a clearer final broth.

4- to 5-pound roasting chicken, cut up
1 stalk celery with top
1 onion, peeled and quartered
  Parsley sprigs
  Salt and freshly ground black pepper
  Cream Noodles (recipe below)
  Hot mashed potatoes

Cover chicken with cold water, heat to boiling, gently boil for 5 minutes, drain and rinse. Put chicken into a large kettle with cold water to cover (about 3 quarts), celery, onion, 1 large parsley sprig, 2 teaspoons salt, and ¼ teaspoon pepper. Cover and simmer until chicken is tender, about 45 minutes to 1 hour. Remove chicken from bones in large pieces. Strain broth and remove excess fat from top. Heat broth to boiling. Add noodles, and boil until tender, about 10 minutes. Return chicken to broth and simmer to heat through. Correct seasoning. Ladle over potatoes. Garnish with parsley sprigs. Makes 6 to 8 servings.

Cream Noodles. In a bowl, beat 1 egg, and beat in 2 tablespoons heavy cream or milk and ½ teaspoon salt. Stirring with a wooden spoon, gradually add enough all-purpose flour to make a stiff dough, about 1 to 1¼ cups. On a floured board, roll out as thinly as possible, turning and dusting with flour occasionally. Dust lightly with flour, and let stand for 20 minutes. With a sharp knife, cut into strips ¼ inch wide and 3 inches long. Spread out and let dry for 2 hours.

SUGGESTED ACCOMPANIMENTS:
Salad of leaf lettuce from the garden sprinkled with uncooked
    fresh peas
Fruity and fresh white table wine, as a dry California Chenin
    Blanc or French Colombard
Fresh strawberries

CARIBBEAN COCONUT CHICKEN
HAITI

If you wish, you can brown the chicken and make it ready for baking slightly ahead of time.

3 whole large frying chicken breasts (about 3½ pounds
    total), split and boned
    Salt and freshly ground black pepper
7 tablespoons butter
2 medium-large sweet onions, very thinly sliced
1 tablespoon brown sugar
    About ¼ teaspoon powdered saffron
1 small jar (2 ounces) sliced pimentos
3 tablespoons dried currants
1½ tablespoons fresh lemon juice
    Coconut crust (recipe below)

Season chicken generously with salt and pepper. Fold loose corners of each piece under to form a compact shape. Heat 4 tablespoons of the butter in a large frying pan over medium heat until it bubbles. Add chicken breasts and sauté until golden on both sides and opaque almost throughout, about 10 to 12 minutes total. Remove and arrange in a single layer in a shallow baking dish. Add remaining 3 tablespoons butter to pan, add onions, and sauté until tender. Stir in ¼ teaspoon salt, the brown sugar, saffron, pimentos, currants, and lemon juice. Spoon over chicken. Cover and bake in a 375° oven for 10 minutes. Remove cover, sprinkle with coconut crust, and continue baking, uncovered, for 10 minutes more. Spoon all juices over chicken as you serve. Makes 6 servings.

Coconut crust. Toss together thoroughly 3 tablespoons melted butter, 1½ tablespoons fresh lemon juice, ¼ teaspoon salt, ¼ teaspoon freshly ground black pepper, ¾ cup flaked coconut, and 3 tablespoons finely chopped fresh parsley.

SUGGESTED ACCOMPANIMENTS:

Buttered corn bread

Salad of butter or Boston lettuce and thin crisp fresh pear slices with oil-vinegar dressing seasoned with a little marjoram and ground cloves

Full and dry white table wine, such as a California Sauvignon Blanc

Unlavish Lamb

Cooks without plenty, over many ages and in many sparse lands of the world, created with lamb and kept their people eating.

I suppose that since lamb was the only meat those cooks had, they developed a wide range of uses within their means to make lamb tasty and satisfying. And what a wealth of wondrous dishes they willed us—lamb couscous, kefta, stuffed grape leaves, fruited lamb stews, lentils and lamb, Niçoise lamb . . . Theirs was high inventiveness. We are lucky to have the chance to fatten our own thin times with lamb ideas from those cooks of other times and places.

ARMENIAN LAMB HAMBURGERS
(Lule Kebab) ARMENIA

The seasonings in this recipe are on the light side; increase them if you wish. Cooks in some locales would season with cumin and oregano instead of coriander.

> 2 *pounds lean ground lamb*
> 1 *cup minced onions*
> 1 *teaspoon salt*
> ½ *teaspoon freshly ground black pepper*
> ½ *teaspoon ground coriander*

Thoroughly mix all ingredients. Shape into 12 football-shaped patties, each about 4 by 2 inches. Thread each on a metal skewer. Grill over medium-hot to hot glowing charcoal (or oven-broil 2 to 3 inches from heat), turning, until brown on all sides and medium-rare or done to your liking. Makes 6 servings.

SUGGESTED ACCOMPANIMENTS:
Rice and/or cracked wheat pilaf
Seasonal fresh vegetables
Light dry red wine

LAMB-AND-CRACKED-WHEAT LOAF
(Kibbi) SYRIA

In this recipe, I have made two small concessions to convenience and to keeping the cost down: (1) Most Syrian cooks would layer the dish before baking with raw lamb and onions, sautéed lamb and onions and nuts, and another layer of raw lamb and onions; but a baked kibbi without layering is also authentic. (2) Pine nuts are the first-choice nut for an accurate kibbi; walnuts are a second choice for the sake of economy.

Unlavish Lamb

If your lamb is extremely lean, add ¼ cup melted butter to it as you mix it for baking.

¾ cup regular cracked wheat
2½ pounds finely ground lean lamb
1 cup very finely chopped onions
1½ teaspoons salt
¼ teaspoon freshly ground black pepper
⅛ teaspoon ground cinnamon
¾ cup chopped walnuts, lightly toasted
¼ cup melted butter

Cover wheat with cold water, let soak for 1 hour, and drain. Thoroughly mix with remaining ingredients except butter. Pat into a buttered 9-inch-square baking pan. Cut through meat to mark 2-inch diamonds or triangles. Pour butter over top. Bake in a 375° oven for 1 hour. Makes 8 servings.

SUGGESTED ACCOMPANIMENTS:
Green beans cooked with tomatoes or artichokes
Dry red table wine

PROVENÇAL LAMB STEW

FRANCE

The springtime flavors of lamb and fresh vegetables in this stew seem to call for two more vegetables as accompaniments: boiled new potatoes in their skins and fresh green beans. Then you can add a lettuce salad with some finely sliced celery and some dill in the oil-and-vinegar dressing. A wine should be a bright young red such as a California Zinfandel. Finish with lemon meringue pie or a fresh-fruit compote including oranges and perhaps pineapple and a fruit sherbet topping, or end with cheese and more red wine.

For a more sumptuous meal, change the meat to one round-bone or shoulder lamb chop per person. Brown chops in their own fat in a heavy kettle, discard any excess fat, and continue as below.

3½ *pounds meaty pieces lamb breast (spareribs), cut*
     between ribs into serving-size pieces
     Salt and freshly ground black pepper
1 *large can (15 ounces) tomato sauce*
1 *can (6 ounces) tomato paste*
1 *cup dry red table wine*
1 *tablespoon olive oil*
3 *large pressed cloves garlic*
2 *cups finely chopped sweet onions*
4 *large carrots, peeled and thinly sliced*

Season lamb very generously with salt and pepper. Place in a single layer in one or two large shallow pans and bake in a 450° oven, turning once, until well browned, about 40 minutes. Remove meat, drain well, and put into a heavy kettle. Mix tomato sauce, paste, wine, oil, and garlic, and pour over meat. Cover and simmer for 30 minutes. Stir in onions and carrots. Cover and simmer for 1 hour more. Taste juices and correct seasoning with salt and pepper. Serve meat with all juices spooned over. Makes 6 servings.

NOTE: As almost always with a stew, this is a little better if you make it ahead of time and reheat it before serving.

DIAMOND MEAT PATTIES
(Köfte) TURKEY

This is one item of excitement at a "meat restaurant" near Istanbul. The patties are studded with melted nuggets of cheese and barbecued. Ground veal may replace the ground lamb.

> *2 or 3 green onions*
> *1 pound lean ground beef*
> *1 pound lean ground lamb*
> *2 tablespoons finely chopped fresh parsley*
> *2 teaspoons salt*
> *½ teaspoon freshly ground black pepper*
> *¼ teaspoon ground cumin*
> *¼ teaspoon crumbled dried oregano*
> *3 pressed cloves garlic*
> *¼ pound natural Gruyère or Emmenthal cheese, cut into*
> *¼-inch cubes*
> *About 1 cup plain yogurt at room temperature*

Mince white part of onions; thinly slice green tops. Mix together thoroughly white part of onions, beef, lamb, parsley, salt, pepper, cumin, oregano, and garlic. Mix in cheese to distribute evenly. Divide mixture into six portions and shape each into a diamond-shaped patty about 6 inches long and 3½ inches wide. Grill over medium-hot to hot glowing charcoal (or oven-broil 2 to 3 inches from heat), turning to brown both sides and allowing about 3 minutes each side for medium-rare. Sprinkle yogurt with onion tops and pass to spoon over meat. Makes 6 servings.

SUGGESTED ACCOMPANIMENTS:
Hot pita bread
Combination salad of marinated white beans, chopped tomatoes, sweet red onions, and salad greens
Full dry red wine
Honey-and-nut pastry

APRICOT-ALMOND TAJINE

Fresh coriander makes a pretty and proper green garnish.

¼ cup butter
¼ cup olive oil
2 large onions, very thinly sliced
2 teaspoons ground ginger
  About 1½ teaspoons salt
  About ½ teaspoon freshly ground black pepper
2 cinnamon sticks
2 large pressed cloves garlic
2½ pounds lean boneless leg of lamb, cut into 1½-inch
  cubes
6 ounces (about 1 cup) moist dried apricots
2 tablespoons honey
2 tablespoons fresh lemon juice
¾ cup finely chopped lightly toasted almonds
  Lemon wedges

In a large, heavy kettle, heat butter and oil over medium heat. Add onions, ginger, salt, pepper, and cinnamon; sauté until onions are golden. Stir in garlic. Add lamb and turn to coat all pieces with onion mixture. Cover and simmer slowly until meat is very tender, about 1½ hours. Stir occasionally. Add apricots to liquid in kettle; cover and cook for 20 minutes more. With a slotted spoon, remove meat to a warm serving platter or plates; arrange apricots over top; keep warm. Add honey to juices in kettle. Cook over high heat, stirring, until reduced to a thin sauce. Stir in lemon juice. Pour over lamb. Sprinkle with almonds. Garnish with lemon wedges, and squeeze on juice to taste. Makes 5 or 6 servings.

Unlavish Lamb

SUGGESTED ACCOMPANIMENTS:
Cucumber and leaf-lettuce salad
Well crusted French bread
Tart dry rosé wine

MIDDLE EAST LAMB AND LENTILS

IRAN

I like to make this dish a day ahead of serving. Then the flavors become fully married, and it is easy to lift off any excess fat that has chilled on top. But you certainly can make it the day of serving.

This topping is optional, but well worth adding for the sweet accent of onions: Sauté about 6 cups chopped onions in about ¾ cup butter until very well browned, and sprinkle over top at serving time. You can also add a garnish of fresh coriander sprigs; this is more important to the dish when you skip the onion topping than when you include it.

Consider the saltiness of your chicken broth as you add salt and pepper to taste.

  *4 lamb shanks, each sawed in half
   About 3 tablespoons olive oil
  3 cups finely chopped onions
  1 green bell pepper, finely diced
  4 large pressed cloves garlic
  2 cups (1 pound) lentils, rinsed
  1 large can (1 pound, 12 ounces) whole tomatoes
  1 tablespoon ground cumin
  ¼ teaspoon ground cinnamon
  2 quarts chicken broth
   About 2 teaspoons salt*

About ½ teaspoon freshly ground black pepper
6 lemons, quartered

In a very large, heavy kettle, brown lamb well on all sides in oil. Add onions and green pepper and sauté until limp. Stir in garlic, lentils, tomatoes, cumin, cinnamon, broth, and salt and pepper to taste. Cover and bake in a 350° oven until meat and lentils are tender, about 2 hours; stir occasionally. Cool, cover, and chill overnight. Lift off and discard excess fat from top. Cover and slowly reheat over direct heat or in a 350° oven. Garnish with lemons, and liberally squeeze on juice to taste. Makes 8 servings.

SUGGESTED ACCOMPANIMENTS:
Fresh leaf spinach
Cucumber salad
Bright red wine

Pork to Pleasure

A favorite wine writer and I have an ongoing discussion about wine and pork. He holds, if I translate him correctly, that pork—in even its most sumptuous mode—can command an excellent wine, but not an exquisite wine. He thinks that the basic character of pork defies the accompaniment of the finest wine. I contend that pork can start out with high credentials, maintain them through preparation, and justify a match with nearly the best from a cellar.

For day in and day out, though, he is right. Most pork dishes are not ultimately refined; much of their appeal derives from the fact that they are so unpretentious. Certainly the pork dishes gathered here are of a homey nature and call for good but not great, delicious but not divine, wines—and even more often for beer. For these recipes it is all to the good that I must bow to the wine man's sense of what is appropriate. Eating and drinking warmly and well is the purpose here.

SZEGEDIN GOULASH

Besides its voluptuous taste, the best traits of this goulash are that it does not need the usual browning of meat and it needs no flour for thickening. Sauté the onions long and well.

> *4 ounces bacon, cut into small pieces*
> *2 large onions, very thinly sliced*
> *About 5 teaspoons paprika*
> *2 pounds boneless lean pork, cut into 1-inch cubes*
> *Salt and freshly ground black pepper*
> *2 teaspoons whole caraway seeds*
> *⅜ teaspoon crumbled dried marjoram*
> *1 large pressed clove garlic*
> *1 large can (1 pound, 11 ounces) sauerkraut, well rinsed and drained*
> *2 cups commercial sour cream at room temperature*
> *Finely chopped fresh parsley*

In a large, heavy kettle over medium heat, cook bacon until cooked through but not crisp. Add onions and sauté until tender and golden. Stir in paprika. Sprinkle pork with 1½ teaspoons salt and ½ teaspoon pepper; add to kettle and turn to coat with onion mixture. Cook for about 10 minutes, turning once or twice. Add caraway, marjoram, garlic, and sauerkraut; and turn to mix. Cover tightly and simmer until meat is very tender, about 2 hours; stir occasionally. Stir in half of the sour cream and just heat through. Correct seasoning if necessary. Sprinkle with parsley. Pass remaining sour cream. Makes 5 servings.

SUGGESTED ACCOMPANIMENTS:
Cold cucumber salad
Dark bread or boiled potatoes
Beer

HONEY-BRAISED PORK AND GREENS, SHANGHAI

Nettie Ho brought this recipe with her when she fled Shanghai in 1950. It makes a mellow dish that is smoothly satisfying. The original recipe calls for green mustard cabbage, available in Oriental markets, but I actually prefer chard cabbage (bok choy). *The wine ingredient may be a Chinese dry white wine or one of our own California dry white table wines.*

Serve with steamed white rice. Add some of the rice to the contents of your soup bowl if you wish.

3½-*pound fresh boneless pork-shoulder-blade Boston roast*
    (boneless pork butt)
    About 2 tablespoons honey
    About 2 tablespoons peanut or other salad oil
¾ *cup dry white table wine*
  3 *tablespoons sugar*
⅛ *teaspoon crushed dried hot red peppers*
    Soy sauce
    Freshly ground white pepper
    About 2½ pounds chard cabbage or about 2 pounds
    Chinese green mustard cabbage or Chinese cabbage or
    mustard greens or spinach or Swiss chard, cut crosswise
    into 1-inch pieces and heavy pieces cut into 1-inch
    squares; or about 2 pounds green head cabbage, cut
    into 1-inch wedges

Place meat in a large, heavy kettle, cover with cold water, heat to boiling; then simmer, covered, for 1 hour. Pour off water. Dry meat and rub surfaces with honey. Heat oil in kettle over medium heat. Add meat and brown well on all sides. Remove any excess fat in kettle. Add wine, sugar, red peppers, 3 tablespoons soy sauce, ½ teaspoon white pepper, and 5 cups cold water. Cover tightly and simmer until meat is very tender, about 2 hours; turn meat occasionally. Remove meat. Heat liquid in kettle to boiling, add greens, and cook until just tender, about 5 to 10 minutes. Serve in individual soup plates: a piece of meat, some greens, and a ladling of broth. Pass more soy sauce and white pepper. Makes 6 servings.

SUGGESTED ACCOMPANIMENTS:
Steamed white rice
Fresh oranges
Light and fruity red wine such as Zinfandel

TOAD IN THE HOLE

GREAT BRITAIN

This dish is a traditional English supper.

1 *pound fresh pork link sausages*
2 *eggs*
1 *cup milk*
½ *teaspoon crumbled dried thyme*
⅜ *teaspoon salt*
¾ *cup sifted all-purpose flour*

Prick each sausage with a fork. In a heavy frying pan 9 inches in diameter over medium heat, lightly brown sausages on all sides. Pour off drippings in excess of 4 to 5 tablespoons. Beat eggs lightly with milk, thyme, and salt; add flour and beat until smooth; pour over sausages. Bake in a 425° oven until puffed and brown, about 25 minutes. Immediately cut and spoon out to serve. Makes 4 servings.

SUGGESTED ACCOMPANIMENTS:
Cold applesauce
Hot tea

FAVORITE SPARERIBS, SHERRY GLAZED
USA

1 *side pork spareribs, about 3 pounds, cracked in half*
   lengthwise and to separate rib ends
   Salt and freshly ground black pepper
1 *can (8 ounces) tomato sauce*
½ *cup honey*
½ *cup dry sherry*
2 *tablespoons wine vinegar*
3 *tablespoons grated onions*
1 *large pressed clove garlic*
½ *teaspoon Worcestershire sauce*

Season ribs generously on both sides with salt and pepper. Place in a shallow roasting pan and bake in a 400° oven for 45 minutes. Drain off accumulated fat. Mix together remaining ingredients and pour over ribs. Reduce oven heat to 350° and bake until ribs are tender, about 40 minutes more; turn once and baste occasionally during baking. Cut into serving pieces. Makes 4 servings.

SUGGESTED ACCOMPANIMENTS:
Fresh corn pudding or corn on the cob
Leaf lettuce and fresh coriander salad
Beer

CARAWAY CABBAGE AND PORK CHOPS
(Essig-Kraut) CZECHOSLOVAKIA

I usually think of horseradish and mustard as going with boiled beef; their use with pork is excellent and the two are nearly required condiments with this dish. I like to make a little mixture of them on my plate and then use the mixture sparingly.

Beer is the obvious answer to what to drink with this meal. A young and fruity red wine, as a California Zinfandel or Gamay Beaujolais, is a less obvious but excellent choice.

4 pork chops cut ¾ inch thick, about 6 ounces each
    Salt and freshly ground black pepper
6 tablespoons butter
1½ cups finely chopped onions
8 cups finely shredded green cabbage
2 pressed cloves garlic
¼ teaspoon caraway seeds
    About 3 tablespoons mild red wine vinegar

Trim excess fat from chops; cook trimmings in a large, heavy frying pan until fat accumulates; discard trimmings. Add chops and brown on both sides over medium-high heat; do not crowd in pan; add a little butter if necessary. Remove from pan and season generously on both sides with salt and pepper. Add butter and onions to pan and sauté onions until limp. Stir in cabbage, garlic, caraway, 1 teaspoon salt, about ½ teaspoon pepper, and vinegar. Sauté until cabbage wilts. Arrange chops on top of cabbage, cover, and simmer until pork is tender, about 15 minutes. Makes 4 servings.

SUGGESTED ACCOMPANIMENTS:
Parsley-buttered boiled potatoes
Beer or a young and fruity red wine
Poached apples or dried apricots

PLUMP PORK PATTIES, WALTER FREY
(Crêpinettes) SWITZERLAND

A proper crêpinette is wrapped in lacy caul fat before browning. But Walter allows the skipping of the caul for the sake of an easier way to arrive at a plump and juicy fresh pork patty.

2 *slices farm-style white bread, crusts removed*
¾ *cup heavy (whipping) cream*
¼ *cup milk*
1 *pound lean boneless pork (trimmed shoulder, butt, loin ends), ground twice with finest blade*
1 *tablespoon brandy*
½ *beaten egg*
2 *tablespoons finely minced green onions (white part only)*
¾ *teaspoon salt*
½ *teaspoon freshly ground white pepper*
¼ *teaspoon each ground nutmeg, ginger, and crumbled dried sage*
⅛ *teaspoon each crumbled dried thyme and bay*
⅛ *teaspoon freshly ground black pepper*
1/32 *teaspoon ground cloves*
About 1 cup fine soft bread crumbs
Butter
½ *cup dry white table wine*
2 *tablespoons brandy*
Watercress

Soak bread in cream and milk, then mash with a fork until smooth. Mix very thoroughly with all except last 5 ingredients. Dipping hands into cold water, shape mixture into 4 patties, each about 3 inches in diameter and 1½ inches thick. Roll in crumbs to coat. Heat about 2 tablespoons butter in a heavy frying pan over medium heat until it bubbles. Add patties, and brown well on both sides, adding more butter as needed, about 20 minutes total. Then bake in a 350° oven for 20 minutes. Remove to warm serving plates; spoon any drippings and loose crumbs over top. Add wine and the 2 tablespoons brandy to pan and cook over high heat, stirring, until reduced to about ⅓ cup. Pass as a sauce for crêpinettes. Garnish each plate with a little bush of watercress. Makes 4 servings.

SUGGESTED ACCOMPANIMENTS:
Well-buttered puréed potatoes sprinkled with chopped watercress
Butter lettuce with a light oil-vinegar-Dijon mustard dressing
Dill wilted cucumbers (optional)
Fruity Alsatian white table wine or a dry and fully flavored
California Gewürztraminer

Beef (and One Veal)

Meat is beef. At least to most Americans it is. Yes, there are pork, lamb, veal, and all those other things. But if we really want meat, we want beef and nothing else. No matter how much we tout the nonbeef items with intent to eat less expensively, we cannot escape our built-in yearning for red-blooded beef.

This is fine. A healthy liking for beef is not a negative thing, but it can be expensive—unless we learn how to shape and direct it. And that goes more so for veal.

CRESS BURGERS BARBECUED

USA

*For supper outdoors, barbecue these watercress-zested beef
patties to put into toasty buns, split French rolls, or broiled
English muffins. Offer Dijon-style mustard, but use only a
little if at all. For a fancier occasion, or for supper indoors,
pan-broil the meat and top it with an elegant little sauce
derived from Portugal* (see next recipe).

2 *pounds ground beef chuck*
1 *teaspoon salt*
   About ½ teaspoon freshly ground black pepper
¼ *teaspoon sugar*
3 *tablespoons minced green onions (white part only)*
½ *cup chopped watercress leaves*

Lightly and thoroughly mix all ingredients together. Shape into
four patties, each about 1 inch thick. Broil over hot glowing
charcoal until done to your liking. Makes 4 servings.

CRESS BURGERS WITH
LEMON-CREAM SAUCE

PORTUGAL

   Salt
   Cress Burgers, uncooked (see preceding recipe)
1 *cup heavy (whipping) cream*
½ *teaspoon Dijon-style mustard*
1½ *tablespoons fresh lemon juice*
   Watercress sprigs

Beef (and One Veal)

Lightly sprinkle salt over bottom of a large, heavy frying pan and place over medium-high heat. When pan is hot, add burgers, brown on both sides, and cook until rare or done to your liking. Remove to serving plates or platter and keep warm. Beat together with a fork the cream, mustard, and lemon juice. Add to frying pan, increase heat to high, and cook, stirring, to loosen drippings and until liquid reduces to consistency of heavy cream. Pour over patties. Garnish with watercress. Makes 4 servings.

BOILED BEEF

Boiled beef is one of the most versatile ways to make a little meat go a long way. Quite often it may merely supplement its delicious and hearty accompanying vegetables, rather than form the main part of the meal, so small meat portions are suitable.

The next three recipes give examples of how to amplify boiled beef in such a way.

The following is the basic recipe for boiling a beef brisket.

3 to 5 pounds beef brisket
1 peeled onion studded with 2 whole cloves
1 stalk of celery with top
1 bay leaf
1 peeled clove garlic
1 tablespoon salt
½ teaspoon freshly ground black pepper

Cover beef with cold water, heat to boiling, boil for 5 minutes, drain and rinse. Place beef in a large kettle with remaining ingredients. Add enough cold water to cover. Heat to boiling, cover, and simmer until meat is very tender, about 3 hours; turn meat once or twice. Drain meat and carve into thin slices across the grain. Makes 5 to 10 servings.

NOTE: The first beef boiling is not vital. But I like to do it to rid the beef of the film that forms on the broth when meats are first boiled and which eventually has to be skimmed off.

SUMMER KOHLRABI

CZECHOSLOVAKIA

This old-time Czech supper shifts its ingredients according to the season. In the summertime, they are kohlrabi and marble-size new potatoes. In the wintertime, they are lentils and larger potatoes. In either season, the potatoes are boiled in their jackets, quickly peeled at serving time, and rolled in butter and parsley.

The plan is to serve thin slices of hot boiled beef with the two vegetables, and offer grated fresh (or prepared) horse-radish and German-style mustard to go with the beef, and pour cold, fully flavored beer.

> 1 cup finely chopped onions
> 1 pound peeled kohlrabi, cut into stick pieces about
>   1¼ inches long and ¼ inch thick
> 4 tablespoons butter
> ½ teaspoon salt
>   About ¼ teaspoon freshly ground black pepper
> 1 tablespoon flour
> 1 cup milk
> ⅓ cup finely chopped fresh parsley

In a heavy frying pan over medium heat, sauté onions and kohl-rabi in butter until well coated with the butter. Sprinkle with salt and pepper. Cover tightly and cook, stirring occasionally, until kohlrabi is tender, about 25 minutes. Sprinkle with flour and turn to mix. Gradually add milk and cook and gently stir mixture until milk thickens to a smooth sauce. Correct seasoning, adding salt and pepper generously. Stir in parsley. Makes 4 servings.

SAVORY LENTILS

CZECHOSLOVAKIA

This is the wintertime accompaniment for the Czech boiled-beef supper described in the preceding recipe.

> 1 *cup finely chopped onions*
> 2 *tablespoons butter or bacon drippings*
> 1 *cup lentils, rinsed*
>   *About 1¾ cups stock from boiled beef or use water*
> 1 *large pressed clove garlic*
> 1 *small bay leaf*
>   *Salt*
> ⅛ *teaspoon crumbled dried marjoram*
>   *Freshly ground black pepper*
>   *About 1 tablespoon mild red wine vinegar*
> 1 *tablespoon finely chopped fresh parsley*

In a kettle, sauté onions in butter until limp. Add lentils, stock, garlic, bay leaf, 1 teaspoon salt, and the marjoram. Heat to boiling, then cover and simmer until lentils are just tender, about 40 to 45 minutes; stir occasionally, and add a little more stock if necessary to keep mixture very moist. Taste and add salt if necessary. Stir in a generous grinding of pepper, the vinegar, and parsley. Makes 4 servings.

NOTE: Any leftover lentils may be used for another economical dish: Sauté the lentils in a little butter or bacon drippings to reheat, then top with a softly fried egg.

A PIEDMONTESE GREEN SAUCE

This refreshing green sauce (salsa verde) *is meant to go over both the beef and its accompanying boiled new potatoes.*

½ slice French-style bread without crust
   Mild red wine vinegar
1 cup olive oil
1 cup finely chopped fresh parsley
¼ cup very finely chopped sweet red onions
3 large pressed cloves garlic
   Salt
¼ teaspoon crushed dried hot red peppers
1 hard-cooked egg, finely chopped

Soak bread in enough vinegar to moisten; squeeze dry and crumble finely; mix into olive oil. Stir in parsley, onions, garlic, 1 tablespoon vinegar, ½ teaspoon salt, red peppers, and egg. Let stand for about 20 minutes. Taste and correct seasoning with a little more salt and vinegar if necessary. Ladle over hot sliced boiled beef and boiled potatoes. Makes about 2 cups, enough for 6 servings.

SUGGESTED ACCOMPANIMENT:
Bright dry red wine, as a Grignolino

ARGENTINE BEEF SAUTÉ

Some Argentineans would serve rice on the side with this dish, but Americans would probably prefer a green salad and hot garlic-buttered French bread.

Beef (and One Veal)

1 *pound lean ground beef chuck*
1½ *cups coarsely chopped onions*
1 *cup coarsely chopped green bell peppers*
1½ *teaspoons salt*
½ *teaspoon freshly ground black pepper*
1 *teaspoon crumbled dried basil*
¼ *teaspoon sugar*
¼ *teaspoon crumbled dried oregano*
⅛ *teaspoon crushed dried hot red peppers (optional)*
3 *large pressed cloves garlic*
2 *tablespoons chopped fresh parsley*
1 *small can (about 8 ounces) red kidney beans*
1 *small can (8 ounces) golden hominy, drained*

In a large, heavy frying pan over medium heat, brown meat in its own fat. Add onions and green peppers and sauté just until limp. Stir in salt, pepper, basil, sugar, oregano, red peppers, garlic, and parsley. Drain beans and save liquid. Add beans and hominy and simmer, uncovered, gradually adding about ¼ cup of the bean liquid, for 10 minutes. Stir occasionally. Makes 4 servings.

SUGGESTED ACCOMPANIMENT:
Dry red table wine

BEEF AND ONION STEW I
(Stefado)   GREECE

This dish is such an old favorite of mine that I could hardly think of writing a cookbook without including it. For this book, I have changed the proportions to use a lesser-than-usual amount of meat and to provide for more of the spicy sauce and protein-rich cheese and nuts. Almost every time that I adjust recipes for lower cost, I find that making more juices and using less meat makes for greater tastiness and, for me, fuller pleasure in eating.

To be properly Greek, you would use the feta cheese, but I prefer a flavorful, meltable Jack.

> 2 large onions, thinly sliced
> ½ cup butter
> 2 pounds lean boneless beef chuck, cut into 1½-inch cubes
> Salt and freshly ground black pepper
> 1 bay leaf
> 2 tablespoons dried currants
> 1 can (6 ounces) tomato paste
> ⅔ cup dry red table wine
> 2 tablespoons mild red wine vinegar
> 1 tablespoon brown sugar
> 2 large pressed cloves garlic
> ½ teaspoon ground cumin
> ¼ teaspoon ground cinnamon
> 1/16 teaspoon ground cloves
> 1 pound natural Jack cheese, diced, or ¾ pound imported feta cheese, crumbled
> About 1 cup walnut halves

In a heavy kettle, sauté onions in butter until tender and golden. Season meat generously with salt and pepper. Add to kettle and turn to coat each piece well with onion mixture. Add bay leaf and currants. Mix tomato paste, wine, vinegar, sugar, garlic, cumin, cinnamon, and cloves, and add to kettle. Cover and simmer slowly until meat is very tender, at least 2 hours. Stir to blend. Sprinkle with cheese and walnuts, and heat just until cheese softens. Makes 4 to 6 servings.

SUGGESTED ACCOMPANIMENTS:
Fresh leaf spinach salad with oil-vinegar dressing
Crusty bread
Dry red table wine

UKRAINIAN MEAT ROLL

RUSSIA

According to Siberian-born O. Alex Kaluzhny, a Russian would give so much credit and attention to a superb pastry and a worthy filling that he would never want a sauce— unless it might be a little melted butter to pour over. Alex explains that the Russian's inclination to savor demands a chance to "work on" the pastry and the filling without other distractions, and he would anticipate a filling that would justify the fine pastry.

In old times in Russia, these meat spirals might have been something to eat during the day with tea. Here we can turn them into a meal.

  Smooth Pastry (recipe below)
  Meat Filling (recipe below)
1 *egg yolk, lightly beaten*
  Warm melted unsalted butter

Roll pastry out to a 15- by 7-inch rectangle on a floured board. Sprinkle to within 1 inch of edges with cooled meat filling. Starting with lengthwise edge, roll up as a jelly roll; turn under ends to seal. Place, seam side down, on an ungreased baking sheet. Gently brush yolk over surface. Bake in a 375° oven until rich golden brown, about 45 to 50 minutes. Cool on a rack to warm or to room temperature before serving. Cut into thick crosswise slices. Offer melted butter. Makes 4 main-course servings.

Smooth Pastry. Sift together into a bowl 1¼ cups sifted all-purpose flour, 1 teaspoon baking powder, and ¼ teaspoon salt. Cut in ½ cup lard until particles are fine. Beat 1 egg with 3 tablespoons milk, add to flour mixture, stir with a fork to mix, and gather into a ball. Wrap in clear plastic wrap, and chill for 8 hours.

Meat Filling. In a frying pan, brown ⅔ pound ground beef

round in 2 tablespoons butter until crumbly. Add ½ cup finely chopped onions, 1 large carrot that has been peeled and coarsely grated, and 1½ teaspoons sugar; sauté until onions are limp. Stir in 3 tablespoons finely chopped fresh parsley, about ¾ teaspoon salt, and about ⅜ teaspoon freshly ground black pepper. Let cool.

SUGGESTED ACCOMPANIMENTS:

Cherry tomatoes
Finely sliced boiled or steamed zucchini
Light beer

FIREHOUSE OVEN POT ROAST

USA

A San Francisco fireman told me of this recipe years ago. I think it is worth passing on because of its good taste and simplicity. You can tend a lot of fires while this is not demanding your attention. Yes, the recipe is correct: there is no browning of meat and there is no salt.

The baking time varies somewhat according to the quality and size of your roast.

4- to 5-*pound boneless pot roast (rump* or *chuck)*
1 *can (8 ounces) tomato sauce*
1 *large pressed clove garlic*
1 *cup dry red table wine*
2 *pieces orange zest (orange part of peel only),*
   each 2 by 1 inch
2 *cinnamon sticks*
4 *whole cloves*
12 *to 24 small (1½-inch diameter) boiling onions, peeled*

Put meat into a large, heavy kettle. Mix tomato sauce, garlic, and half of the wine and pour over. Add orange zest, cinnamon, and cloves. Cover tightly and bake in a 300° oven for 2½ to 3 hours. Add remaining wine and the onions. Cover and bake until onions and meat are tender, about 1 hour more. Remove meat and onions to carving or serving platter. Discard zest, cinnamon, and cloves. Tip kettle to make a deep well of juices; skim off fat. Stir juices to blend and ladle lightly over carved meat slices. Makes 6 to 8 servings.

SUGGESTED ACCOMPANIMENTS:
Green peas
A California Burgundy

BEEF AND ONION STEW II
(Stefado)   GREECE

This Stefado does not begin with the usual braising of beef. It allows simply settling the meat into melted butter and letting the long, low simmering do the browning.

  3 *pounds lean beef chuck, cut into 1½-inch cubes*
    Salt and freshly ground black pepper
½ *cup butter*
  2 *pounds small white boiling onions (about 1½ inches in diameter), peeled*
  1 *can (6 ounces) tomato paste*
½ *cup dry red table wine*
  2 *tablespoons red wine vinegar*
  1 *tablespoon brown sugar*
¼ *teaspoon ground cumin*
  1 *pressed large clove garlic*
  1 *bay leaf*
  1 *cinnamon stick*
½ *teaspoon whole cloves*
  2 *tablespoons dried currants*

Wipe meat dry. Season generously with salt and pepper. Melt butter in a heavy kettle with cover. Add meat and turn to coat each piece well with butter, but do not brown. Arrange onions over meat. Mix tomato paste, wine, vinegar, sugar, cumin, and garlic; pour over onions. Add bay, cinnamon, cloves, and currants. Cover kettle. Simmer very slowly until meat is very tender, about 3 hours; do not stir. As you serve, stir juices to blend to a sauce. Makes 6 servings.

SUGGESTED ACCOMPANIMENTS:

Heavily sesame-seeded crusty bread or French-style bread with lightly toasted sesame-seed butter

Full-flavored dry red table wine, such as a California Petite Sirah or a red Rhone

CANTONESE BLACK BEANS, PUMPKIN, AND BEEF

CHINA

This dish is colorful and rich-tasting and is unusual even to many Cantonese. In the United States, Cantonese cooks use winter squash when pumpkin is not available. You can do the same. Buy the pungent fermented black beans (also called preserved black beans, black salted beans, or Dow See) in a Chinatown, an Oriental market, or a supermarket with a specialty food section.

½ *pound beef flank or bottom round steak, sliced across the grain into strips no thicker than* ⅛ *inch*
    Soy sauce
  1 *tablespoon cornstarch*
  ¾ *teaspoon sugar*

1½ *pounds fresh pumpkin* or *winter squash such as*
    butternut, banana, or Hubbard
4 *teaspoons fermented black beans, well washed and*
    drained
1 *large pressed clove garlic*
2 *tablespoons peanut* or *other light salad oil*
    Boiling water
1 *tablespoon cornstarch mixed to a smooth paste with*
    1 *tablespoon water*
3 *tablespoons thinly sliced green onions with part of*
    green tops

Toss steak strips with 1½ tablespoons soy sauce, the 1 tablespoon cornstarch, and ¼ teaspoon of the sugar; set aside. Peel pumpkin and cut into 1-inch cubes. Crush beans in a mortar with pestle or in a bowl with back of a spoon and mix in garlic to make a paste; stir in 2 tablespoons soy sauce and remaining ½ teaspoon sugar. Heat oil in a large, heavy frying pan or wok over high heat. Add beef and sauté quickly, turning just to barely brown; do not cook through; turn out of pan. Reduce heat to medium. Add to frying pan the pumpkin, black-bean mixture, and ½ cup boiling water. Cover and cook just until pumpkin is tender, about 15 minutes; if necessary to keep pumpkin very juicy, add a little more water during cooking. Return beef to frying pan along with enough of the cornstarch paste to thicken liquid in pan and to coat meat and vegetables. Toss to heat through. Turn into serving dish, sprinkle with onions, and serve immediately. Offer more soy sauce. Makes 3 main-dish servings or 4 to 6 servings as part of a Chinese dinner.

SUGGESTED ACCOMPANIMENTS:
Cantonese stir-fried green beans
Steamed rice
Dry rosé wine or beer

DEVILED SHORT RIBS

USA

I like deviled beef ribs tremendously, but they never have enough meat for me. So I give a similar treatment to short ribs, and I get to revel in the full meatiness and flavor along with the deviled effect.

6 *pounds beef short ribs, cut into serving pieces*
  Salt and freshly ground black pepper
1 *large onion, coarsely chopped*
  About ⅓ cup water
  About 2 tablespoons red wine vinegar
  About 2 tablespoons melted butter
  Fine soft or fine dry bread crumbs
  Chopped fresh parsley
  Red wine vinegar or lemon wedges

Arrange ribs in a single layer in a heavy casserole or baking pan. Bake in a 425° oven for 30 minutes; turn once. Pour off accumulated fat. Season meat generously with salt and pepper. Add onion and water. Cover and bake in a 350° oven until meat is tender, about 1½ hours; if necessary to prevent burning, add a little more water. Discard onion and pan juices. Sprinkle meat surfaces with vinegar, brush with butter, and coat with crumbs. Continue baking, uncovered, until crumbs are crisp, about 30 minutes. Sprinkle generously with parsley. Sprinkle with vinegar or lemon juice to taste as you eat. Makes 6 to 8 servings.

SUGGESTED ACCOMPANIMENTS:
Buttered leaf spinach
Peeled cucumbers quartered lengthwise
Dry red table wine, as a California Burgundy
Sliced oranges or poached dried apricots or lemon meringue pie

A BEEF BURGUNDY
(Boeuf Bourguignonne)   FRANCE

I once made this with beef round instead of chuck. It was a mistake. You need the looser texture of chuck for this.

This is a slightly more saucy Bourguignonne than most, so it offers the possibility of sharing its full-flavored juices with potatoes or crusts of bread for dipping. I also find this a little more refined than many versions.

Make this a day ahead of serving if you can; the flavors are sure to be fuller than when just completed.

2½ *pounds lean boneless beef chuck, cut into* 1½-*inch cubes*
¼ *cup butter*
2 *cups finely chopped onions*
1 *pound fresh mushrooms, sliced* ⅛ *inch thick*
2 *large pressed cloves garlic*
4 *teaspoons tomato paste*
⅓ *cup flour*
1¼ *cups beef broth* or *stock*
¾ *teaspoon salt*
¾ *teaspoon crumbled dried thyme*
¾ *teaspoon crumbled dried basil*
⅜ *teaspoon freshly ground black pepper*
1 *very large bay leaf*
½ *cup dry sherry*
3½ *cups full-flavored dry red table wine*
   About 2 *tablespoons finely chopped fresh parsley*

In a large, heavy kettle over medium-high heat, brown meat in butter (do not crowd). Remove meat and reduce heat to medium. Add onions to kettle, and sauté until limp. Add mushrooms and sauté for about 5 minutes. Add garlic. Whisk together tomato paste, flour, and broth, and add to kettle; cook and stir until mixture is blended and juices begin to boil and thicken. Stir in salt, thyme, basil, pepper, bay leaf, the beef, sherry, and all except 2 tablespoons of the red wine. Cover tightly and simmer very slowly until meat is very tender, about 3 hours; stir occasionally. Correct seasoning with salt and pepper. Just before serving, stir in remaining 2 tablespoons red wine. Serve in shallow soup plates or deeply rimmed dinner plates. Sprinkle with parsley. Makes 5 or 6 servings.

SUGGESTED ACCOMPANIMENTS:
Boiled potatoes or crusty French bread
Lettuce salad with cooked and chilled fresh green peas
Full flavored dry red table wine

FLANK STEAK TERIYAKI

JAPAN

Although it is suggested here that you grill the steak, you can also oven-broil it about 2 inches from heat and 3 minutes each side for rare. Make a small cut in steak to check doneness.

⅓ *cup soy sauce*
¼ *cup salad oil*
3 *tablespoons dry sherry*
2 *tablespoons honey*
1 *very large pressed clove garlic*
¼ *cup finely chopped green onions with part of green tops*
1½ *teaspoons minced or grated fresh ginger*
1 *flank steak, about 1½ pounds (not scored)*
Toasted sesame seeds (optional)

Combine all ingredients except steak and sesame seeds to make a marinade. Pour over steak and let stand at room temperature for 2 hours (or covered and chilled for 4 hours); turn steak occasionally. Grill steak over very hot glowing charcoal, turning once, until done to your liking, about 4 minutes each side for rare; baste occasionally with marinade. Carve into very thin slices, cutting on the diagonal from top to bottom of steak. Sprinkle carved slices with toasted sesame seeds if you wish. Offer additional soy sauce. Makes 4 servings.

SUGGESTED ACCOMPANIMENTS:

Hot white rice
Cooked seasonal green vegetable, as green beans, asparagus,
    spinach, broccoli, Chinese edible-pod (sugar) peas
Dry red table wine
Cold fresh oranges

AVOCADO CHILI

USA

Among the chilies of my acquaintance, this is more American than Mexican, but more Mexican than most American versions. For best flavor, make this ahead and reheat later for serving.

1½ *pounds ground beef chuck*
1½ *cups finely chopped onions*
    About 4 teaspoons chili powder
    Salt and freshly ground black pepper
2 *teaspoons dry mustard*
½ *teaspoon sugar*
½ *teaspoon ground cumin*
2 *pressed cloves garlic*
1 *large can (1 pound, 12 ounces) peeled tomatoes, broken up*
1 *can (about 1 pound) red kidney beans, drained*

4 teaspoons finely grated unsweetened baking chocolate
1 large ripe avocado, peeled and thinly sliced lengthwise

In a large, heavy kettle over medium heat, brown meat in its own fat. Add onions and sauté until limp. Stir in chili powder, 2 teaspoons salt, ½ teaspoon pepper, the mustard, sugar, cumin, garlic, tomatoes, and beans. Cover and simmer for 20 minutes, stirring occasionally. Stir in chocolate. Taste and correct seasoning. Ladle into warm shallow bowls. Arrange avocado over top, and sprinkle with salt. Makes 5 or 6 servings.

SUGGESTED ACCOMPANIMENTS:
Hot corn tortillas or toasted corn bread
Broken iceberg lettuce with oil and vinegar dressing, with
    fresh coriander leaves if possible
Fresh oranges and/or pineapple
Beer

INDIVIDUAL BEEF POT ROASTS WITH CHEESE-CRUMB PASTA

ITALY

For a pretty presentation, heap pasta in center of large warm serving dish. Surround with shanks and artichokes in sauce.

If bacon begins to overbrown as shanks brown, remove it and return after meat is browned.

3 slices bacon, cut into small pieces
6 meaty beef shank slices, ½ pound each
    Wine-tomato sauce (recipe below)
2 packages (9 ounces each) frozen artichoke hearts, thawed
    Cheese-crumb pasta (below)
    Finely chopped fresh parsley

In a large heavy frying pan over medium heat, cook bacon until some fat accumulates. Add shanks, and brown lightly on both sides. Pour off any excess fat. Pour wine-tomato sauce over beef. Cover and simmer slowly until meat is very tender, about 1 hour and 45 minutes; stir occasionally. Add artichoke hearts, tucking them beneath liquid. Cover and simmer until tender, about 15 minutes. Gently stir liquid to blend. Correct seasoning with salt. Serve meat, artichokes, and sauce with pasta. Sprinkle very lightly with parsley. Makes 6 servings.

Wine-tomato sauce. Stir together 1 can (14 to 16 ounces) stewed tomatoes (large pieces cut up), 2 cans (6 ounces each) tomato paste, 1¼ cups water, ½ cup dry red table wine, 2 teaspoons sugar, 1½ teaspoons crushed fennel seeds, 1½ teaspoons salt, 2 finely crushed bay leaves, 1 large pressed clove garlic, and 2 teaspoons grated fresh lemon peel.

Cheese-crumb pasta. In a small frying pan over medium heat, sauté ¾ cup fine soft fresh bread crumbs in 3 tablespoons butter until lightly toasted. Cook 6 ounces *mafalde* (narrow ripple-edged noodles) or lasagne noodles, broken into 4-inch lengths, *al dente* in boiling salted water with a little olive oil. Drain well. Toss with crumbs. Sprinkle with 3 tablespoons grated Romano cheese.

SUGGESTED ACCOMPANIMENTS:
Romaine salad with oil–vinegar–black-pepper dressing
Dry red table wine, such as a California burgundy
Chilled sliced oranges and cinnamon-spiced sugar cookies

SWEDISH MEATBALLS

SWEDEN

I got this recipe for "authentic Swedish meatballs" from a Danish lady in Copenhagen, and with no apology for the

Japanese soy sauce. I choose not to question the origin of any part of the recipe because I like the outcome.

If necessary, you can brown the meatballs a little ahead of time, then cover and reheat in the oven before adding to the sauce.

½ *cup fine soft bread crumbs*
½ *cup milk*
¾ *pound lean beef*
¼ *pound fat pork meat*
 2 *ounces baby beef liver*
 1 *egg, beaten*
  Salt and freshly ground black pepper
  Crumbled dried basil, marjoram, rosemary, and thyme
½ *cup finely minced onions*
  Finely chopped fresh parsley
  About ½ *cup butter*
½ *pound fresh mushrooms, thinly sliced*
¼ *cup beef broth*
 1 *cup commercial sour cream*
 2 *teaspoons Japanese soy sauce*

Soak crumbs in milk. Using medium-sized blade on meat grinder, grind together beef, pork, and liver (or coarsely chop in a food processor). Mix together thoroughly the meat mixture, crumbs and milk, egg, ¾ teaspoon salt, ¼ teaspoon pepper, ⅛ teaspoon *each* basil, marjoram, rosemary, and thyme, the onions, and 1 tablespoon parsley. Dipping hands into cold water, shape mixture into balls about 1 inch in diameter. Heat about 4 tablespoons butter in a large, heavy frying pan over medium heat until it bubbles; add meatballs and brown on all sides. As meatballs are browned, remove from pan with a slotted spoon and keep warm; add more butter as needed. Add enough butter to pan to make about 2 tablespoons drippings in pan. Add mushrooms and sauté until tender; remove from pan and keep warm. Add to frying pan the broth, ⅛ teaspoon pepper, and ¹⁄₁₆ teaspoon *each* basil, marjoram, rosemary, and thyme. Cook and stir to loosen drippings in bottom of pan. Remove from heat, add sour cream and soy sauce and stir until smooth. Add a little more sour cream and soy sauce if you like a very generous saucing. Return meatballs and mushrooms to pan, and gently turn over low heat just until heated through. Sprinkle with additional parsley. Makes 6 servings.

SUGGESTED ACCOMPANIMENTS:

Buttered sliced carrots
Lingonberries or whole cranberries in sauce
Boston or butter lettuce salad
Red wine

SPINACH-STUFFED VEAL BREAST
(Cima) ITALY

To many San Francisco Northern Italians, the mention of cima *brings to mind a grandiose picnic, a gathering of many families, an all-day affair. The food on such an occasion is elaborate and abundant, and the anticipated highlight is the stuffed veal breast. It is served cold, and each carved slice is a slender rib bone holding veal meat and a custardy spinach filling.*

But cima *is not relegated to picnics alone. In many homes, it is the traditional Sunday company roast. Then it is served hot, and the just-carved slices are presented prettily fanned out on a big serving platter.*

1 *veal breast (about 3 pounds) with pocket for stuffing*
Salt and freshly ground black pepper
Spinach Stuffing (recipe below)
¼ *pound bacon slices*

Sprinkle veal surfaces with salt and pepper to season. Spoon stuffing lightly into pocket, distributing it evenly. Close with small skewers. Place in a shallow roasting pan, bone side down. Arrange bacon over top. Bake in a 325° oven for 1½ hours. Allow to stand for 30 minutes before carving into slices, cutting between bones. Makes 6 servings.

Spinach Stuffing. Cut ⅓ pound fresh Italian garlic pork sausages from casings and finely crumble. In a heavy frying pan over medium heat, lightly brown sausages in their own fat. Discard any fat in excess of 1 tablespoon. Add ⅓ cup minced green onions (white part only) and sauté until limp. Stir in ¼ cup finely chopped fresh parsley. Let cool. Cook 1 pound fresh leaf spinach (weighed with coarse stems removed) until just tender, drain, finely chop, squeeze very dry, and let cool. Slightly beat 3 eggs with 1 teaspoon ground sage, a generous grinding of black pepper, and ⅓ cup freshly grated Parmesan cheese. Stir in sausage mixture and spinach.

SUGGESTED ACCOMPANIMENTS:
Sliced ripe tomatoes
Bread sticks or crusty bread
Dry red wine

Variety Meats:
More Wondrous Than Curious

I am not looking forward to the day when nearly everyone thinks that variety meats are just the nicest things ever. Then those delicious items will be more costly. And then there will not be so many available for the likes of you and me. So I am not inclined to urge you toward learning to like such delicacies as tongues, livers, gizzards, and so on. But if you already have an appetite for these, you may enjoy the following recipes.

PAN-BROILED LIVER
WITH PARSLEY BUTTER

FRANCE

This is a succulent dish if you like liver rare. Otherwise, I do not recommend it.

Liver takes a lot of salt. Do not fear to add it. Be sure that you get baby beef liver, not costly calf's liver.

About 2 teaspoons each *olive oil and butter*
1 *slice baby beef liver cut* 1½ *inches thick*
(about 1 *to* 2 *pounds)*
Salt and freshly ground black pepper
¼ *to* ½ *cup butter*
½ *to* 1 *teaspoon fresh lemon juice*
2 *to* 4 *tablespoons finely chopped fresh parsley*

Heat the 2 teaspoons each of oil and butter in a heavy frying pan over medium heat. Add liver and brown well on one side. Turn and cook on second side until liver is rare, about 15 minutes total (if necessary, make a small cut to check doneness). Remove to a warm platter and keep warm. Season well with salt and pepper. Remove excess fat from frying pan, leaving brown drippings. Add the ¼ to ½ cup butter and heat until it foams and begins to brown; stir in lemon juice and parsley. Slice liver thinly. Pour hot butter sauce over. Serve slices with all juices. Makes 3 to 6 servings.

SUGGESTED ACCOMPANIMENTS:
Cooked fresh leaf spinach
Burgundy-style dry red table wine

TONGUE IN SPANISH SAUCE

SPAIN

3- to 4-pound fresh beef tongue
1 peeled onion studded with 3 whole cloves
1 stalk celery with leaves
1 bay leaf
¼ teaspoon whole black peppercorns
1 tablespoon salt
  Spanish Sauce (recipe below)

Put tongue into a kettle with cold water to just cover; add remaining ingredients except sauce. Heat to boiling, then simmer until tongue is tender, about 3 to 3½ hours. While hot, remove skin from tongue and trim off excess root tissue. Return tongue to broth to reheat if necessary or to keep warm until serving time. Slice tongue, and pass sauce to ladle over. Makes 6 to 8 servings.

Spanish Sauce. Beat together well with a fork ½ cup mild white wine vinegar, ½ teaspoon salt, ¼ teaspoon freshly ground black pepper, 1 cup olive oil, 2 tablespoons minced green bell peppers, 2 tablespoons minced fresh red bell peppers or canned pimientos, 2 tablespoons minced fresh parsley, 1½ tablespoons minced green onions (white part only), 2 teaspoons minced capers, and 2 hard-cooked eggs, finely chopped. Correct seasoning with salt and pepper.

SUGGESTED ACCOMPANIMENTS:
Fresh spinach with or without a little bacon
Full dry white wine

GREEN-PEPPERCORN PATE

FRANCE

Splurging for green peppercorns (now widely available in specialty food and spice stores) would not be justified if you served this as a first course. But if you spread the pâté thickly over hot toasted French bread slices and side with a salad and white wine, you make a grand small meal, and not at all out of budget bounds.

I credit Daniel Bouché of the bistro Au Petit Montmorency in Paris with the idea of a green-peppercorn first course. (His robustly satisfying creation was actually a terrine of sweetbreads.) This pâté is smooth and nutty-tasting until you encounter the spicy bite of green peppercorns.

2 tablespoons butter
½ pound chicken livers
¼ pound fresh mushrooms, thinly sliced
¼ cup minced green onions with part of green tops
   About ⅜ teaspoon salt
⅓ cup dry white table wine
1 whole bay leaf
1 small pressed clove garlic
¼ teaspoon dry mustard
¼ teaspoon crumbled dried tarragon
⅛ teaspoon crumbled dried rosemary
¼ cup soft butter
4 teaspoons drained green peppercorns
   Parsley sprig (optional)

Melt the 2 tablespoons butter in a frying pan. Add livers, mushrooms, onions, and salt; sauté for 5 minutes. Add wine, bay leaf, garlic, mustard, tarragon, and rosemary. Cover and simmer for 15 minutes or until livers are tender. Uncover and continue cooking until most of the liquid has disappeared. Remove bay leaf.

Put mixture into a blender container along with the soft butter and whirl until nearly smooth. Taste and add salt if necessary. Mash half of the peppercorns with a fork; fold into mixture along with the remaining 2 teaspoons whole peppercorns. Turn into a crock. Cover and chill for 8 hours or more. Garnish pâté with additional peppercorns *or* a sprig of parsley. Makes about 1⅓ cups or 4 servings.

SUGGESTED ACCOMPANIMENTS:
Hot toasted French bread slices
Very thinly sliced ham or prosciutto (optional)
Ripe tomatoes
Green salad
Dry white table wine or Champagne

COUNTRY CAPTAIN GIZZARDS

USA

James Beard once suggested making a Country Captain entirely of chicken gizzards instead of with chicken pieces. The idea appealed to me immediately, and especially when that dear and great food authority rolled off his description of such a fine "ragout of gizzards."

¼ *cup all-purpose flour*
1 *teaspoon salt*
¼ *teaspoon freshly ground black pepper*
1 *pound chicken gizzards, all fat removed, well washed, and drained*
About 4 tablespoons butter
⅓ *cup finely chopped onions*
⅓ *cup finely diced green bell peppers*
About 1½ teaspoons curry powder
½ *teaspoon crumbled dried thyme*

1 *can (14½ ounces) stewed tomatoes*
1 *large pressed clove garlic*
3 *tablespoons moist dried currants*
   About ⅓ cup blanched toasted almonds

Mix flour, salt, and pepper in a paper bag. Add gizzards and shake to coat with mixture. In a large, heavy frying pan, brown gizzards on all sides in butter. Remove gizzards. Reduce heat to low. Add to pan the onions, green peppers, curry, and thyme; cook and stir to loosen brown drippings. Add tomatoes and garlic. Return gizzards to pan. Cover tightly and bake in a 325° oven until tender, about 45 minutes. Stir in currants. Pass almonds to accompany. Makes 3 or 4 servings.

SUGGESTED ACCOMPANIMENTS:
Hot steamed or boiled white rice
Salad of thinly sliced oranges and green or sweet onions and
   shredded red radishes on a bed of leaf lettuce, with an oil-lime
   juice dressing poured over
Cold beer

GLOSSED CHICKEN LIVERS ON A BED OF GREEN BEANS

USA

Sometimes I like to pasta-sauce vegetables—for fewer calories or just for a change. However, the saucing for this recipe also goes well on fresh fettuccine (about 12 ounces of it).

   About ⅓ cup butter
1 *pound chicken livers, rinsed and dried*
1 *teaspoon salt*
½ *teaspoon freshly ground black pepper*

⅔ *cup minced green onions with part of green tops*
⅓ *pound thinly sliced fresh mushrooms*
⅓ *cup dry white table wine*
  2 *large ripe tomatoes* or 2 *canned whole tomatoes, peeled,*
     seeded, and finely chopped
  6 *tablespoons minced fresh basil leaves* or ¾ *teaspoon*
     crumbled dried basil
  ½ *teaspoon minced fresh rosemary* or *crumbled dried*
     rosemary
  2 *large pressed cloves garlic*
1½ *cups heavy (whipping) cream*
1½ *pounds whole Italian (Romano) green beans, ends*
     trimmed, or *fresh string beans that have been French-cut*
     and cut into 2-inch lengths
  3 *tablespoons finely chopped fresh parsley*

In a large, heavy frying pan, heat butter over medium heat until it bubbles and begins to brown. Add livers and brown on all sides, about 5 minutes total. Remove livers from pan with slotted spoon and sprinkle with salt and pepper. Add onions and mushrooms to pan and sauté until tender. Add wine, increase heat to high, and cook and stir to loosen drippings and until wine is completely reduced. Return livers to pan along with tomatoes, basil, rosemary, garlic, and cream. Gently boil until liquid reduces to consistency of heavy cream. Correct seasoning, adding salt and pepper generously. Meantime, cook beans, uncovered, in boiling salted water until just tender, drain well, and lightly salt. Turn livers over beans. Sprinkle with parsley. Makes 4 servings.

NOTE: If your fresh tomatoes are not ruby-ripe, add ¼ to ½ teaspoon sugar.

SUGGESTED ACCOMPANIMENTS:
Green salad
Italian bread
Fruity dry white table wine, as a full flavored Riesling
Fresh nectarines or peaches

ELLIOTT LIVER

USA

Bob Elliott is the finest home barbecue chef I know. He has a highly tuned sense of how to handle whatever item he is cooking, whether it is a whole salmon, a saddle of lamb, or a hamburger. His wife complements all that with an extraordinary talent for combining seasonings in an original way. The skills of both show up here.

Be sure to have a deep and hot bed of coals for barbecuing. You can grill this as done as you wish, but I think it tastes best rare, for then it is buttery. Watch carefully. Once it begins to cook, liver transforms quickly from blood-rare to done.

1¼ *cups dry red table wine*
¾ *cup beef broth*
2 *tablespoons salad oil*
1 *tablespoon each wine vinegar and fresh lemon juice*
½ *cup minced green onions with part of green tops*
½ *cup finely chopped fresh parsley*
1 *bay leaf, crumbled*
1 *teaspoon crumbled dried thyme*
1 *teaspoon salt*
½ *teaspoon each crumbled dried basil, oregano, tarragon, and rosemary*
2 *pounds baby beef liver sliced* 1½ *inches thick*

Combine 1 cup of the wine and remaining ingredients except liver in a saucepan. Heat to boiling, then simmer for 2 minutes. Let cool, add remaining wine, and pour over meat. Cover and refrigerate for 24 hours; turn meat once or twice. Return to room temperature before cooking. Place meat on grill above a deep bed of glowing hot charcoal. Grill on one side for 4 minutes, dip into marinade, grill on second side for 4 minutes; repeat until done to your liking, about 15 minutes total for rare. Make a small cut in meat if necessary to check for doneness. Carve diagonally into ¼-inch-thick slices. Makes 4 to 6 servings.

NOTE: To oven broil, place liver on rack in shallow roasting pan. Broil about 4 inches from heat, turning and basting as above, for about 15 minutes total for rare.

SUGGESTED ACCOMPANIMENTS:
Rice and kidney bean casserole or green rice
Orange-slice salad
Light red table wine, as a California Burgundy
An almond dessert

Pancakes for Supper

Some of these recipes are for full-meal pancakes. Many of them are for big-dessert pancakes. They are all large and lush. And the idea about them is that they give a good excuse for a big dessert for supper and not much else beforehand—maybe just a strong hot beef bouillon or a vegetable-and-broth soup. This idea is a custom in many lands. The Swedes have their traditional supper of split-pea-and-ham soup and thin lingonberry pancakes. The Germans have eggy omelet pancakes served with a dried fruit compote. The country Swiss make big apple oven pancakes. In Berkeley, California, Mrs. Joseph Henry Jackson used to entertain on Sunday nights with cheese-filled blintzes served with apricot jam and sour cream, and pots of tea.

Pancake suppers give good nutrition and taste contentment without the need for much costly meat protein.

LAYERED HAM PANCAKES
(Rakott Sonkáspalacsinta)   HUNGARY

These are refined, their ingredients simple.

1½ *cups commercial sour cream*
¼ *teaspoon Dijon-style mustard*
2 *tablespoons finely minced green onions (white part only)*
½ *pound cooked well-smoked ham, ground (about*
    2 cups ground ham)
    About ¼ teaspoon salt
    Freshly ground black pepper
    Crêpes (recipe below)
1 *tablespoon butter*

Stir together 1 cup of the sour cream, the mustard, onions, ham, salt, and a generous grinding of pepper. Place 1 crêpe on a buttered baking plate. Spread with a thin layer of the ham mixture. Repeat, using all of the ham mixture and ending with a crêpe. Dot with butter. Bake in a 350° oven until heated through, about 25 minutes. Garnish top with spoonfuls of the remaining sour cream which has been stirred smooth. Cut into wedges. Makes 4 servings.

Crêpes. Beat 3 eggs slightly. Add 6 tablespoons flour and ⅜ teaspoon salt, and beat until smooth. Add 1 cup milk and beat until smooth. (Cover and chill for ½ to 1 hour if possible; stir well before using.) For each crêpe, heat about ½ teaspoon butter over medium-high heat in a 7- or 8-inch crêpe pan. Pour in about 3 tablespoons batter; quickly tilt and rotate pan so batter covers bottom. When lightly brown on bottom, turn and lightly brown on second side. Makes about 12 crêpes.

SUGGESTED ACCOMPANIMENTS:
Very thinly sliced oranges and a few tomatoes, or dill-wilted
    cucumbers
A fruity Riesling or Gewürztraminer

CAULIFLOWER CRÊPES
(Karfiol Omeletten) SWITZERLAND

*These sauced crêpes make the meal. You might begin it with
a cup of broth and end with a few more crêpes filled with
apricot jam or currant or plum jelly and dusted with powdered sugar.*

1½ *recipes* Crêpes (recipe on page 189)
   2 *tablespoons butter*
      Cauliflower Cream Sauce (recipe below)
      Minced fresh parsley

Roll up crêpes and arrange in a single layer in a buttered shallow
baking dish. Dot with butter. Bake in a 350° oven until heated
through, about 8 to 10 minutes. For each serving, arrange 4 or 5
crêpes over half of a warm plate, and ladle sauce alongside;
sprinkle lightly with parsley. Makes 4 servings.

Cauliflower Cream Sauce. Thinly slice ¾ pound cauliflower
flowerets lengthwise through flower and stem. In a large, heavy
saucepan, sauté ½ cup minced green onions (white part only) in
¼ cup butter until tender. Stir in 3 tablespoons flour, 1 teaspoon
salt, ½ teaspoon freshly grated or ground nutmeg, and ⅛ teaspoon freshly ground white pepper to make a smooth paste.
Gradually add 3 cups milk, cooking and whisking to make a
smooth slightly thickened sauce; simmer, whisking, for 5 minutes.
Cook cauliflower, covered, in a small amount of boiling salted
water just until tender, about 3 to 5 minutes; drain well. Fold
into sauce.

SUGGESTED ACCOMPANIMENT:
Fresh and fruity white wine

SWEDISH OVEN PANCAKE

SWEDEN

I first learned of this grandiose northland pancake in a recipe published in a western home magazine years ago. It became an irreplaceable favorite of mine. But I always had to take it on faith that the recipe was truly Swedish—until I got to Sweden to find out for myself. It is.

4 *thin slices bacon, cut into small pieces*
1 *cup sifted all-purpose flour*
2 *tablespoons sugar*
¾ *teaspoon salt*
3 *eggs*
2 *cups milk*
1 *to* 1½ *cups heavy cream, softly whipped*
  About 1 *cup lingonberry preserves or*
  whole cranberries in sauce

In a heavy frying pan about 10 inches in diameter, cook bacon until crisp. Do not pour off any drippings unless in excess of 4 tablespoons. Meantime, sift together flour, sugar, and salt. Beat eggs lightly with milk; add to sifted ingredients and beat until smooth. Pour batter over bacon in hot frying pan. Bake in a 375° oven until set and golden brown, about 30 minutes. Cut into wedges and serve immediately. Top with cream and lingonberries. Makes 4 to 6 servings.

BRITTANY BUCKWHEAT CREPES

FRANCE

In Brittany, these buckwheat pancakes would be baked on a giant griddle, but here you can bake them handily in a crêpe pan. The Breton beverage, and the really right one, is cold apple juice or cider.

If buckwheat flour is not available in your supermarket, shop for it in a health-food store.

> 1 *egg*
> 1 *cup milk*
> ½ *cup commercial buttermilk*
> 1½ *teaspoons sugar*
> ½ *teaspoon salt*
> ¾ *cup stirred buckwheat flour*
> ¼ *cup sifted all-purpose flour*
> ¼ *cup melted butter*
>   *Butter*

Slightly beat egg. Beat in milk, buttermilk, sugar, and salt. Gradually add buckwheat and white flours, beating to make a very smooth batter. Cover and let stand at room temperature for 1 hour. Beat in melted butter. For each crêpe, heat about ½ teaspoon butter over medium-high heat in a 7- or 8-inch crêpe pan. Pour in about 3 tablespoons batter; quickly tilt and rotate pan so batter covers bottom. When brown on bottom, turn and brown on second side. Makes about 12 crêpes.

NOTE: Add a little more milk if necessary in order to make a batter thin enough to flow over bottom of pan to make a thin crêpe. You can stack these crêpes and hold them in a warm oven for a little while as you bake more.

NOTE: For a main dish, place an egg that has been softly fried in butter and seasoned with salt, and pepper if you wish, in center of baked crêpe. Fold in two sides of the crêpe to cover egg, and top with a spoonful of room-temperature sour cream. Serve additional crêpes with melted butter and sour cream. (The sour cream is to suit my tastes, not necessarily a Breton's.)

RUSSIAN FRIED CHEESE CAKES
(Sirniki)   RUSSIA

These butter-browned patty cakes should be rather neutral-tasting so that they require something with a tang for a topping—sour cream stirred with a little granulated or brown sugar or kirsch or other liqueur to sweeten if you wish. The sirniki do not have to be hot when served, just fully warm. The sour cream must be room temperature, not chilled.

The cheese must be dry-curd (uncreamed) cottage cheese, often called baker's cheese. It is usually available in Russian or Jewish delicatessens or bakeries, or you can sometimes order it from a creamery.

Serve these for lunch, with fruit, such as poached apples or plums, and tea. Or serve them as a supper dessert with soup preceding. A Russian's likely choice for the soup would be borscht or pelmeni soup.

    1 *pound dry-curd cottage (baker's) cheese*
    2 *egg yolks, slightly beaten*
1½ *tablespoons all-purpose flour*
    1 *tablespoon sugar*
      About 1 *teaspoon salt*
      Flour
      Butter
      Powdered sugar
      Commercial sour cream at room temperature, stirred smooth

Using a wooden spoon, force cheese through a fine sieve into a bowl. Stir in egg yolks, flour, sugar, and salt. Drop dough by slightly heaping tablespoonfuls into a mound of flour on a board, roll in flour, and shape into cakes about 2½ inches in diameter and ½ inch thick. Lightly cross-score on both sides with a floured dinner knife. Heat a generous amount of butter in a heavy frying pan over medium-high heat until it bubbles. Add cakes and cook until rich golden brown and a little crisp on both sides. Arrange on serving platter or plates and sprinkle generously with powdered sugar stirred through a strainer. Offer sour cream. Makes about 12 cakes or 4 servings.

VONNAS CRÊPES

FRANCE

These crisp-edged circlets are almost frothy with their eggy lightness. They are the three-generation specialty of the restaurant owner, Georges Blanc, who makes them just as his grandmother did when she invented them years ago.

In the Blanc restaurant, the crêpes are served as a separate course after the meat, and are offered with both coarse salt and sugar to sprinkle over. You make your choice. Remarkably, both go well with the crêpes. For a pancake supper after a soup starter, I suggest the crêpes with sugar.

1 *pound mature (baking) potatoes, peeled, sliced, cooked*
   in boiling salted water until tender, and drained
⅓ *cup milk*
¾ *teaspoon salt*
¼ *cup sifted all-purpose flour*
3 *whole eggs*
3 *egg whites*
½ *cup heavy (whipping) cream*
   Clarified Butter (see below)
   Granulated sugar

Beat potatoes to mash. Gradually beat in milk and salt to make a smooth purée. Chill to cool. Beat in flour. Beat in eggs and whites one at a time. Gradually add cream, beating well to make a light mixture. Heat a generous amount of butter in a large, heavy frying pan over medium-high heat. Spoon batter by measuring tablespoonfuls into hot butter, spreading to 3-inch circles. When well browned and crisp-edged on one side, turn and brown well on second side. Offer sugar. Makes 4 to 5 dozen crêpes, 6 dessert servings or 8 accompaniment servings.

Clarified Butter. Slowly melt butter in a small pan over very low heat. Tip pan to make a deep well of butter. Skim off and discard foam that rises to top. Pour or ladle off the clear butter from the milky residue at bottom of pan.

NOTE: You can hold baked crêpes in a warm oven for a few minutes while you bake more. To keep them crisp, do not stack.

POWDERED-SUGARED PANCAKE FLAPS

GERMANY

These little pancake squares appear almost as browned custardy flat pillows. They are quite delicate, not at all husky.

If you have two large pans, you can double the recipe and use both pans at once in order to serve flaps to more people.

2 *eggs*
2 *teaspoons sugar*
⅜ *teaspoon salt*
4 *tablespoons flour*
⅔ *cup milk*
5 *tablespoons butter*
Powdered sugar
Fresh lemon wedges

Slightly beat eggs with sugar and salt. Add flour and beat until smooth. Add milk and beat until smooth. Place a heavy frying pan 10 to 11 inches in diameter over medium heat. Add 3 tablespoons of the butter and heat until bubbling but not browning. Pour in egg mixture. Cook until bottom is set and well browned, about 10 minutes. Cut pancake into long 1- to 1½-inch-wide strips. Turn with a flexible spatula and cook on second side until well browned. Cut crosswise to make squares. Melt remaining butter and pour over squares, gently toss, and bake in a 350° oven for about 10 minutes. Turn squares onto warm serving plates. Sprinkle lightly with powdered sugar and garnish with lemon wedges. Pass additional powdered sugar. Squeeze on lemon juice to taste. Makes 2 servings.

SUGGESTED ACCOMPANIMENTS:
Very thin ham slices
Dried fruit compote

APRICOT PLUMP PANCAKE ROLLUP
HUNGARY

Each serving is a fat log of heady riches.

   2 *eggs*
½ *teaspoon salt*
¼ *cup sifted all-purpose flour*
½ *cup milk*
   2 *tablespoons butter*
      Apricot Filling (recipe below)
¼ *cup commercial sour cream at room temperature,*
      stirred smooth
   2 *tablespoons minced walnuts*
   2 *teaspoons sugar*

Slightly beat eggs with salt. Add flour and beat until smooth. Add milk and beat until smooth. Heat butter in a large, heavy frying pan 10 to 11 inches in diameter over medium-high heat until butter bubbles. Add batter. Transfer to a 350° oven and bake for 25 minutes. With a flexible spatula, gently loosen pancake and slip onto serving platter. Spread with apricot filling. Roll up as a jelly roll. Spoon sour cream over top. Sprinkle with nuts and sugar. Cut crosswise into 3 pieces. Serve immediately. Makes 3 servings.

Apricot Filling. Cook 4 ounces moist dried apricots in water to barely cover until very tender; drain. While hot, add ¼ cup sugar and stir vigorously with a spoon to make a rough purée.

SUGGESTED ACCOMPANIMENT:
Goulash soup and light beer preceding

APPLE PANCAKE PIE

USA

Half of the puffed pancake is folded over the apples to form a sugared-top-crust effect.

You can make the softly spiced apple filling while the pancake bakes. You might want to use kitchen shears to cut the pie into portions.

2 *eggs*
½ *cup milk*
¼ *teaspoon salt*
½ *cup sifted all-purpose flour*
3 *tablespoons butter*
4 *tablespoons sugar*
   Apple Filling (recipe below)

Beat eggs with milk and salt; add flour and beat just until batter is smooth. In a heavy frying pan 10 to 11 inches in diameter, melt 1 tablespoon of the butter to coat bottom of pan. Pour in batter. Bake in a 450° oven for 15 minutes; as soon as center of batter puffs up, prick with a fork; repeat as necessary. Reduce oven heat to 350° and bake for 10 minutes more. Remove from oven. Melt remaining 2 tablespoons butter, pour evenly over pancake, and sprinkle with 2 tablespoons of the sugar. Spoon hot apple filling over half of the pancake. Fold remaining half of pancake over top. Sprinkle with remaining 2 tablespoons sugar. Cut into 4 wedges and serve immediately. Makes 4 large servings.

Apple Filling. Peel 4 tart cooking apples, quarter, core, and thinly slice crosswise. In a large frying pan over medium heat, sauté apples in 6 tablespoons butter for 5 minutes. Mix 6 tablespoons sugar, ¼ teaspoon ground cinnamon, and ⅛ teaspoon ground nutmeg; sprinkle over apples. Cover and cook over low heat for 5 minutes. Uncover and cook for 5 minutes more, turning occasionally (increase heat if necessary to cook most of the juices into apples).

CHERRY SCHMARREN
(Kirschschmarren) AUSTRIA

Royal Anne are the best cherries to use, but you can use Bing.

You can halve this recipe and bake it in an 8- or 9-inch frying pan; it will make one generous dessert.

    2 *eggs*
    2 *teaspoons granulated sugar*
    ¼ *teaspoon salt*
    ¼ *cup flour*
    ⅔ *cup milk*
    1⅓ *cups rinsed and dried whole Royal Anne cherries*
    3 *tablespoons butter*
        Vanilla Powdered Sugar (recipe below)
        Slender lemon wedges

Slightly beat eggs with sugar and salt. Add flour and beat until smooth. Add milk and beat until smooth. Stir in cherries. Place a heavy frying pan 10 to 11 inches in diameter over medium heat. Add butter and heat until bubbling but not browning. Pour in egg mixture, spreading cherries evenly. Cook until bottom is set and well browned. With a pancake turner, cut wedge-shaped pieces of the pancake and turn over to brown on second side. Increase heat to medium-high. Cut wedges into smaller strips about ¾ inch wide. Then turn and cut almost with abandon to get all sides of pieces well browned. Turn onto warm serving plates. Sprinkle generously with vanilla powdered sugar. Garnish with lemon wedges and squeeze on a little juice if you wish. Makes 3 dessert servings.

Vanilla Powdered Sugar. Bury a split vanilla bean in 2 cups powdered sugar, cover tightly, and let stand for 24 hours or more.

CARAMELIZED NORMAN CRÊPES
(Crêpes Normandes Caramelisées)   BELGIUM

In Belgium, this dish would most likely be served at teatime —around five in the afternoon. Here, I fit it into the supper scheme as a big dessert pancake. You can also serve it for breakfast or brunch with fresh raspberries, thinly sliced ham or prosciutto, and coffee.

2 *tablespoons butter*
  Crêpe-Omelet Batter (recipe below)
1 *tart cooking apple, peeled, cored, and cut into*
  ¼-*inch-thick lengthwise slices*
6 *tablespoons sugar*
  Caramel Syrup (recipe below)
  Fresh raspberries (optional)

Place a heavy frying pan 10 to 11 inches in diameter over medium-high heat. Add 1 tablespoon of the butter and heat until bubbling but not browning. Tilt pan to cover bottom with butter. Add batter. Arrange apple slices evenly over top. Dot with remaining 1 tablespoon butter. Sprinkle with the sugar. Transfer to a 350° oven and bake for about 25 minutes. With a flexible spatula, gently loosen pancake. Cut into quarters and lift onto two warm serving plates. Drizzle caramel syrup over top in a fine stream. Serve with a few fresh raspberries on the side if desired. Makes 2 servings.

Crêpe-Omelet Batter. Slightly beat 2 eggs with ½ teaspoon salt. Add ¼ cup all-purpose flour and beat until smooth. Add ½ cup milk and beat until smooth.

Caramel Syrup. Heat together in a small heavy pan over medium heat 2 teaspoons butter and 3 tablespoons sugar. Cook and stir until mixture melts, blends, turns a rich caramel brown, and just begins to smoke slightly and smell a little burned, about 10 minutes.

NOTE: Time the making of the caramel syrup so that you can pour it over the crêpe-omelet just as both are finished. Wait for a few moments before eating to allow the pancake to cool a little and the caramel to set. The caramel forms a crackly clear-amber drizzle.

OVEN-ROASTED SWEET CHEESE CAKES
AUSTRIA

I sometimes make apricot crêpes, too, and offer them along with these cheese crêpes. Then people can eat both kinds and contrast a fruit crêpe with a mellow cheese one. To make apricot crêpes: Spread crêpes with tart apricot jam, roll up as below, dot with butter, bake as below, and sprinkle with vanilla powdered sugar.

Pancakes for Supper

The less served beforehand, the better. But you might want to serve a platter of mild cold cuts with cucumbers, lettuce, and thinly sliced buttered light pumpernickel or rye bread. Then if you have an off-dry fruity white wine with the cold cuts, you can continue it with the crêpes. Regardless of the forerunner to dessert, you need to plan for at least three crêpes per person.

8 *ounces cream cheese, softened*
3 *tablespoons soft butter*
⅓ *cup granulated sugar*
½ *teaspoon vanilla*
⅛ *teaspoon salt*
1 *teaspoon grated fresh lemon peel*
4 *tablespoons plumped golden raisins*
12 *crêpes* (recipe, page 189)
¾ *cup heavy (whipping) cream*
  Vanilla powdered sugar (recipe, page 199) or
  plain powdered sugar

Beat together thoroughly the cheese, butter, granulated sugar, vanilla, and salt. Fold in lemon peel and raisins. Spread center of each crêpe with one-twelfth of the cheese mixture. Fold in two sides, then roll up crêpe. Arrange crêpes, side by side, in a buttered shallow baking dish. Slowly and evenly pour cream over crêpes. Bake in a 350° oven until bubbling, about 10 to 15 minutes. Lift to serving plates. Spoon cream over. Sprinkle with powdered sugar. Makes 12 cakes or 4 servings.

NOTE: To plump raisins, cover with hot water, let stand for 5 minutes, and squeeze dry.

Desserts That Do for Dinner

I have long held that dessert is too great to come at the end of a meal. It deserves more attention. I think that the build-up for dessert should be a carefully nurtured anticipation—not a lot of other eating.

Here is the chance to do right by that concept of dessert. Give a dessert full honor by plotting the menu for it and by intending to eat a lot of it. Let it be much more than an unneeded tail end to a meal. I think that the way to do justice to a glorious dessert is to prepare for it with a little time for anticipation, a directed appetite, and something quite light to eat beforehand. The anticipation should be such that you feel a pleasing sense of eagerness, but not a frantic urgency to eat. It will not do to be famished.

The food that precedes a supper dessert should be something light, perhaps with a glass of wine. Whatever it is, it should serve the role of an appetizer. It should not be discountable, though; it must be in keeping with the worthiness of the dessert; and that means that it must be of value and of interest. It should be a pleasantry to prepare you for even grander pleasures. This something that beckons you to a supper dessert has to vary with the dessert. Usually the best thing for me is a light soup with a clear broth base, such as a mellow lettuce soup seasoned with a hint of ham, or Chinese egg flower soup, or a very petite petite marmite. Or

I like a julienne of fresh vegetables salad, or a lovely pile of just-cooked fresh beans or leaf spinach, or a giant soft butter-lettuce salad. Bigger eaters can begin with something like a bowl of minestrone, a fresh chicken-and-corn chowder, oyster stew, a chef's salad, an omelet, or a platter of cold meats and cheeses with raw-vegetable garnish.

You come by the economy of this meal plan in much the same way as suggested previously for big-dessert pancake suppers: get a lot out of dessert, so that the rest of the meal can be lighter and leaner and less costly than usual.

BARB'S BLUEBERRY TART

USA

You can serve this delicious tart as soon as it's made, or chill and serve up to eight hours later. If you decide to chill the tart, spread on the sour cream no longer than three hours before serving time, and then let it stand at room temperature for about fifteen minutes before serving.

2 *cups fresh blueberries*
  Shortbread crust (recipe below)
1 *jar (10 ounces) or* 1 *cup red currant jelly*
1 *cup commercial sour cream*
2 *tablespoons finely chopped and very lightly toasted walnuts*

Rinse blueberries, drain and dry well. Spread berries over bottom of baked crust—higher along the sides to make a cup in the center. Slowly heat jelly until it melts. Stir to cool slightly. Spoon evenly over berries. Chill until jelly sets well. Stir sour cream until smooth; spread evenly over the center berries, leaving a ring of ungarnished berries along the sides. Chill for 1 to 3 hours (if longer, do not spread sour cream until 1 to 3 hours before serving). Just before serving, sprinkle nuts around the edge of the sour cream to make a decorative border. Makes 6 generous dessert servings.

Shortbread crust. Sift 1 cup unsifted all-purpose flour and 2 tablespoons unsifted powdered sugar into a bowl. Cut in ½ cup butter until particles are fine. Chill for 30 minutes. Turn into a 9-inch tart pan with removable bottom or pie pan. Press firmly into bottom and sides. Bake in 425° oven until golden brown, about 8 to 12 minutes. Cool on a rack.

PARISIAN APPLE CRISP

FRANCE

You want to bake this shortly before serving, but with one adjustment, you can assemble it as long as three hours ahead of baking: toss apple slices with about 2 tablespoons each fresh lemon juice and sugar.

 2 *pounds tart cooking apples*
1⅓ *cups sugar*
 1 *cup sifted all-purpose flour*
 ¼ *teaspoon ground cinnamon*
 ⅔ *cup chopped almonds*
 ½ *cup melted butter*
 ¾ *teaspoon vanilla*
  About 1½ *cups unsweetened heavy cream,*
  softly *whipped*

Peel, quarter, and core apples and cut into ½-inch-thick lengthwise slices. Spread over bottom of a buttered round shallow baking dish, about 9 inches in diameter and 2-quart capacity (or equivalent). Sift together the sugar, flour, and cinnamon. Stir in almonds. Mix butter and vanilla, add to almond mixture, and toss with a fork to make a crumbly mixture. Sprinkle evenly over apples. Bake in a 375° oven until topping is richly browned, about 30 to 35 minutes. Partially cool on a rack. Spoon out to serve. Top each serving with a generous amount of cream. Makes 4 supper or 6 dessert servings.

BREAD PUDDING AFTER THE COACH HOUSE

USA

"Bread Pudding" is really something far more ethereal than the plain name would indicate. There you might have a chance to embellish it with softly whipped cream and a vivid but well-toned raspberry sauce. But I prefer the pudding absolutely pure.

8 *thin slices (about ½ pound) French bread (not sourdough) or Italian bread or farm-style white bread, at least 1 day old*
¼ *cup soft butter*
4 *eggs*
2 *egg yolks*
¾ *cup sugar*
½ *teaspoon ground cinnamon*
⅜ *teaspoon ground nutmeg*
⅛ *teaspoon salt*
1½ *teaspoons vanilla*
3 *cups milk*
⅔ *cup heavy (whipping) cream*
Powdered sugar

Trim crusts from bread. Spread each slice with butter. Arrange, buttered side up, in a buttered 2-quart soufflé or other baking dish. Beat together eggs, yolks, sugar, cinnamon, nutmeg, salt, and vanilla. Scald milk and cream, and gradually beat into egg mixture. Pour over bread. Set baking dish in a pan with hot water about 1 inch deep in bottom. Bake in a 375° oven until nearly set and a silver knife inserted near center comes out clean, about 45 to 50 minutes. Cool on a rack to lukewarm or room temperature. Sift powdered sugar very generously over top. Slip under broiler until sugar melts and glazes. Cool for a few minutes. Spoon into serving dishes. Makes 5 or 6 supper servings or 8 dessert servings.

OMAHA APPLE ROLLUPS

USA

This dessert is rich and homespun, and especially right on a nippy fall night. I remember it as supper sometimes in my childhood, preceded by Mother's very clear and uncluttered vegetable-and-beef soup.

½ *cup granulated sugar*
½ *cup firmly packed light brown sugar*
1 *cup water*
¼ *teaspoon each ground cinnamon and nutmeg*
½ *cup butter*
1 *cup sifted all-purpose flour*
1 *tablespoon granulated sugar*
1 *teaspoon baking powder*
½ *teaspoon salt*
   About ⅓ cup milk
2 *large tart cooking apples, peeled, cored, and coarsely grated (or cut into eighths and very thinly sliced)*
   Heavy (whipping) cream

Combine the ½ cup granulated sugar, the brown sugar, water, cinnamon, and nutmeg in a saucepan. Boil for 5 minutes. Add half of the butter, stir to melt, and set aside to cool to warm. Sift together into a bowl the flour, the 1 tablespoon sugar, the baking powder, and salt. Cut in remaining ¼ cup butter until particles are fine. Sprinkle with milk, and toss with a fork just to moisten. Gather into a ball. On a lightly floured board, knead dough about four times. Roll out to a 13- by 10-inch rectangle. Spread apples over dough. Starting at lengthwise edge, roll up as a jelly roll. Cut crosswise into 12 slices. Place slices, cut side up, in an 8-inch-square baking pan. Pour sugar syrup evenly over. Bake in a 425° oven until rich golden brown, about 45 to 50 minutes. Allow to cool in pan for a few moments. Spoon out and serve while warm. Pass cream to pour over. Makes 4 supper or 6 dessert servings.

BROILED STRAWBERRY AMBROSIA

USA

Serve this dessert just as soon as the crust cools enough to be crisp, so that the fruits will be hot against the cold ice cream.

2 *large ripe bananas, sliced* 3/8 *inch thick*
1 *cup halved or quartered strawberries*
2 *oranges, peeled and cut into bite-size pieces*
1 *tablespoon fresh lemon juice*
1 *cup firmly packed light brown sugar*
6 *tablespoons melted butter*
2/3 *cup sliced almonds*
    Vanilla ice cream

Toss together bananas, strawberries, oranges, and lemon juice. Turn into a 10-inch oven-glassware pie plate or equivalent. Stir together sugar, butter, and almonds; sprinkle over fruits. Broil 6 to 8 inches from heat until sugar melts and almonds lightly toast. Cool for a few moments. Tap crust to break. Spoon into dessert dishes. Top or side with ice cream. Makes 3 or 4 supper servings or 6 dessert servings.

MINCEMEAT-STRAWBERRY SCONE SHORTCAKES

AUSTRALIA

This may call up remembrances of strawberry shortcake. Homemakers in Australia bake these scones especially in December, because for a short season, traditional mincemeat time and prime berry time coincide.

4 *cups sliced fresh strawberries*
½ *cup sugar*
2 *cups sifted all-purpose flour*
4 *teaspoons baking powder*
½ *teaspoon salt*
6 *tablespoons butter*
2 *eggs*
¼ *cup milk*
3 *tablespoons soft butter*
1 *cup prepared mincemeat*
1 *teaspoon grated fresh lemon peel*
1 *tablespoon sugar mixed with* ¼ *teaspoon ground cinnamon*
2 *cups heavy cream, softly whipped and lightly sweetened with sugar*

Gently mix berries with ¼ cup of the sugar (or sugar to sweeten), and let stand for about 30 minutes. Into mixing bowl, sift together flour, the remaining ¼ cup sugar, the baking powder, and salt. Cut in the 6 tablespoons butter until particles are fine. Slightly beat eggs with milk, add to flour mixture, and toss with a fork to make a soft dough. Turn onto a lightly floured board, knead lightly, and divide in half. Roll out each half to a 9-inch circle. Place one circle on an ungreased baking sheet. Spread with 2 tablespoons of the soft butter. Mix mincemeat and lemon peel, and spread over butter. Top with second dough circle, spread with remaining butter, and sprinkle with cinnamon-sugar. With a floured knife, score top into 6 or 8 wedge-shaped pieces. Bake in a 425° oven until well browned, about 18 to 20 minutes. Cut into wedges and serve while still warm. Pass strawberries and cream to spoon over top. Makes 6 supper servings or 8 generous dessert servings.

FRESH CRANBERRY CRUNCH WITH VANILLA CREAM

USA

A pound of cranberries would seem to indicate a lot of cranberries, but they do not go far when people begin eating this dessert. Even when served at the end of a dinner party, this may utterly vanish—as if vacuumed up—before only four diners. The note I wrote on this recipe to myself says, "Never serve to more than four."

I could eat this dessert for breakfast on any cold fall morning—not only because of my unlikely breakfast preferences, but because it offers a wholesome balance of fruit, cereal, and cream. That is not what I am recommending here. I am only testifying to how much I like this dessert, but I can assure you that if you should ever be so fortunate as to have some left over after dinner, it is excellent the next morning cold, with heavy cream over the top.

This is also easy and fast to put together.

1 *pound (4 cups) cranberries, rinsed and well drained*
1⅓ *cups granulated sugar*
2 *tablespoons grated fresh orange peel*
¾ *cup fresh orange juice*
¾ *cup old-fashioned rolled oats*
½ *cup firmly packed dark brown sugar*

⅓ *cup sifted all-purpose flour*
⅓ *cup butter*
  1 *cup heavy cream, softly whipped with 2 tablespoons*
    granulated sugar and seeds scraped from a 3-inch piece
    of vanilla bean

Put cranberries, granulated sugar, orange peel, and juice in a 1½-quart soufflé dish or equivalent. Stir to mix well. Combine oats, brown sugar, and flour in a bowl. Cut or rub in butter to make a crumbly mixture. Sprinkle evenly over cranberries. Bake in a 375° oven until topping is rich golden brown, about 35 to 40 minutes. Cool on a rack until warm. Spoon out and serve with whipped cream. Makes 3 supper servings or 4 generous dessert servings.

SUGGESTED ACCOMPANIMENT:
Coffee

DATE COUSCOUS

MOROCCO

As a child, I found cream of wheat quite fine eating on a cold winter's morning, maybe mainly because of the slightly salty butter melting over the top of that steamy wheaty cereal. The dish rose to greater majesty on those mornings when I found pieces of moist sweet dates as hidden surprises at the bottom of the bowl.

An echo of those early delights drifts over this dessert of North Africa, a great favorite there. (It happens to be good for breakfast, too.) When served in Morocco, the sugar might have a little cinnamon with it, and hot milk would replace the cream suggested here.

You can purchase couscous in many supermarkets and in

specialty food stores handling Middle Eastern, French, or North African products.

> 2 *cups water*
> 2 *tablespoons butter*
> 1/2 *teaspoon salt*
> 1 *cup couscous*
> 3/4 *cup moist pitted dates, coarsely cut into lengthwise pieces*
> 4 *tablespoons melted butter*
>   *Sifted powdered sugar*
>   *Heavy (whipping) cream*

Heat water, the 2 tablespoons butter, and salt to boiling in a heavy saucepan. Gradually add couscous, stirring with a wooden spoon. Continue boiling and stirring until water is almost absorbed, about 2 minutes. Stir in dates, remove from heat, cover tightly, and let stand for 10 to 15 minutes. Fluff with a fork. Spoon into dessert plates. Drizzle with melted butter. Sprinkle lightly with powdered sugar. Pass cream and additional sugar to add to taste. Makes 4 supper or 6 dessert servings.

RHUBARB YORKSHIRE

USA

This rhubarb original resembles a French fresh-fruit cla-foutis, except for more puff and crust and a double-rich topping—yet it hails from Wisconsin.

> 2 *eggs*
> 3/4 *cup milk*
> 1/2 *teaspoon salt*
> 3/4 *cup sifted all-purpose flour*
> 1/4 *cup butter*

½ *pound rhubarb, cut into* ¾-*inch pieces*
   Brown Sugar Topping (recipe below)
   Heavy (whipping) cream

Beat eggs with milk and salt. Add flour and beat until smooth. Heat butter in a 9-inch pie pan in a 425° oven until it bubbles. Immediately pour in egg mixture. Drop rhubarb over center of batter. Bake in a 425° oven until batter is puffed and brown, about 25 minutes. Spoon-cut into wedges and serve in dessert dishes. Top each serving with a big spoonful of warm sugar topping and a generous pouring of cream. Makes 4 to 6 servings.

   Brown Sugar Topping. In a small saucepan, melt ⅓ cup butter. Stir in 1 cup firmly packed light brown sugar and heat just enough to make a thick syrup.

BUTTER SOUFFLE
OF APRICOT NOODLES

HUNGARY

Though sweet pastas do not seem strange at all to Hungarians, they do give a jolt to many Americans. This recipe provides an easy introduction to the whole idea of sweet pastas.

   The butter-and-yolks mixture forms a golden self-saucing throughout the soufflé.

  7 *tablespoons butter*
  2 *cups milk*
  ⅛ *teaspoon salt*
10 *tablespoons sugar*
  2 *ounces dry wide egg noodles (about* 1¼ *cups)*
  6 *tablespoons ground walnuts*
  3 *eggs, separated*

⅛ *teaspoon cream of tartar*
½ *teaspoon vanilla*
¼ *cup apricot jam*
 1 *teaspoon grated fresh lemon peel*
  Heavy (whipping) cream

Heat 1 tablespoon of the butter, the milk, salt, and 3 tablespoons of the sugar over direct heat in top of double boiler until boiling. Add noodles. Place over boiling water and cook, stirring occasionally, until noodles are very tender. Let cool, and drain off any milk not absorbed. Dust bottom and sides of a well-buttered 1½-quart baking dish with 4 tablespoons of the walnuts. Beat egg whites with cream of tartar until foamy, then gradually add 3 tablespoons of the sugar, beating until whites are stiff but not dry. Separately, beat remaining 6 tablespoons butter with 3 tablespoons of the sugar, the yolks, and vanilla until light and fluffy. Fold in noodles. Spoon half of the noodle mixture into baking dish. Dot with half of the jam, and sprinkle with half of the lemon peel. Gently spread with half of the whites. Top with remaining noodle mixture, jam, peel, and egg whites (spread completely to edge). Sprinkle with remaining 2 tablespoons walnuts and remaining 1 tablespoon sugar. Bake in a 350° oven until set and golden, about 30 to 35 minutes. Let cool for a few moments. Spoon into dessert dishes while warm. Offer cream. Makes 3 or 4 supper servings or 6 dessert servings.

OVERSIZE ICE-CREAM PUFFS
WITH DARK CHOCOLATE SAUCE

USA

8 *large Cream Puff Shells* (recipe below)
1 *quart hand-packed vanilla ice cream, slightly softened*
  Dark Chocolate Sauce (recipe below)

Powdered sugar
About ½ cup lightly toasted sliced almonds

Split each shell, fill with ice cream, and place in a shallow dessert plate. Drizzle with warm chocolate sauce. Sift powdered sugar over top. Sprinkle with nuts. Makes 8 servings.

Cream Puff Shells. Combine in a saucepan 1 cup water, ½ cup butter, 1 teaspoon sugar, and ¼ teaspoon salt, and bring to a boil. Add 1 cup sifted all-purpose flour all at once; then beat with a wooden spoon over low heat until mixture leaves sides of pan and forms a mixture that does not separate, about 1 minute. Remove from heat. Continue beating to cool mixture slightly, about 2 minutes. Add 4 eggs, one at a time, and beat after each addition until mixture has a satinlike sheen. Spoon onto a buttered baking sheet, making 8 mounds placed about 2 inches apart. Bake in a 400° oven until golden and lightweight, about 35 minutes. Remove to rack to cool.

Dark Chocolate Sauce. Combine in a heavy saucepan 1½ cups sugar, 3 tablespoons butter, 4 ounces (4 squares) unsweetened baking chocolate, and 1 cup heavy cream. Cook and stir over medium heat until mixture blends and comes to a boil. Then gently boil without stirring for 5 minutes. Remove from heat, and stir in 1 teaspoon vanilla. Makes about 2 cups.

NOTE: To be extra lavish, you can spoon a bed of whipped cream into each dessert plate and set the puff into it. For the cream, beat together 2 cups heavy cream, ¼ cup sugar, and 1½ teaspoons vanilla until very softly whipped.

Index

Index

Index

Index

Index

Recipes by Nation of Origin

Recipes by Nation of Origin